Path to Freedom!

From Birth, Labor Camps, & a New Life

A Cuban Family Memoir by
Nery Barnet Kircher

Halo
PUBLISHING
INTERNATIONAL

ISBN: 978-1-61244-935-7
LCCN: 2020921262

Halo Publishing International, LLC
8000 W Interstate 10, Suite 600
San Antonio, Texas 78230
www.halopublishing.com

Printed and bound in the United States

First, to my husband and sons for
their insistence that I write my memoirs.

To all of those who have suffered under communism
and have lost their lives under this doctrine.

To the Cubans who think the way I think
and are still enduring the grip of the dictatorship.

To all of those who believe in God first and in
Freedom of Speech,
Freedom of Religion,
and Freedom of Assembly.

May the Lord bless you and keep you free!

Contents

Chapter

1

I was born in Cuba, the largest island of the Caribbean Sea. My beautiful island has the shape of a cayman, with a majestic topography that, when he discovered it, made Christopher Columbus say, "It is the most beautiful land that human eyes have ever seen." It is also called the Key to the Gulf of Mexico by many others. The story of my life on the jewel of this island can be characterized by before Castro; after Castro, when it became a Marxist-Leninist communist country; the years my father and I spent in forced labor camps; and when we arrived in the USA. I will try to relate some of the things that are still vibrant in my memory.

Cuba, when I lived there, had six provinces: Pinar del Rio, La Habana, Matanzas, Las Villas, Camagüey, and Oriente. Years after 1971, during Castro's dictatorship, Cuba was divided into fifteen provinces: Pinar del Río, Artemisa, La Habana, Mayabeque, Matanzas, Cienfuegos, Villa Clara, Sancti Spíritus, Ciego de Ávila, Camagüey, Las Tunas, Granma, Holguín, Santiago de Cuba, Guantánamo, and the special municipality of Isla de la Juventud (Isla de Pinos before).

My parents' families were middle class, and when my parents got married, my father worked very hard to be the provider while my mother stayed at home taking care of the children. Both of them had a formal education. My father was a bookkeeper, my mother a piano teacher.

My father's family, the Barnets and Verriers, lived in Pueblo Nuevo for years. Pueblo Nuevo is a suburb located between two gyratory bridges off the city of Matanzas, before the suburb of La Playa. In that town was the Hershey Train Station, where my grandfather was the chief.

My mother's family, the Gonzálezes and Martínezes, lived in La Playa. My grandfather had a "bodega" first, then a distribution van, and he was also a politician.

My parents had a beautiful double wedding. My mom, Elena María—people called her María, but we called her Mima—married my dad, Antonio. People called him Ñico, but we called him Pipo. Juan, my mother's brother, married one of his first cousins, Herminia. They got married at St. Vincent de Paul's Catholic school church. My mom graduated from that school. She wanted her children to go there too. The nuns loved my mother and made her a beautiful wedding veil and bouquet.

After their wedding, my parents moved with my father's parents. They lived in a small house that had a living room, a small room where my Uncle Gonzalo slept, and two bedrooms, one for my two aunts and the other one for my grandparents. At the end of those two bedrooms was another room, which was used as a dining room when I was growing up, along with the kitchen and a bathroom. All of those rooms had beautiful Spanish tile flooring and doors and windows to the courtyard. I don't have any idea where my parents slept when they moved in after their honeymoon. Maybe

10

in the dining room, and maybe the family room was used for dining. Because the place was too small, my parents felt uncomfortable; therefore, they found a house to rent in the same area, just a few blocks from his parents, and moved there. By the way, my grandparents lived at San Juan de Dios #68, next to Simeon Hardware Store.

My grandparents, the Barnet-Verrier family, lived a block and a half from the San John the Baptist Catholic Church in Pueblo Nuevo, where my cousins from my father's side, all of the Barnet girls, and even my grandmother were baptized. We used to go to the church's park and play. Wichi, one of our cousins, lost an eye as a child at this park, when one of the other kids threw a stone and hit him in the eye. We were all devastated when that happened.

My father worked at La Casa Verde for a Spaniard named Cirilo while attending Professional Commerce School, which was before he got married. He began sweeping the store floors first, and as he progressed at his job, my father eventually became Cirilo's general partner and received a high percentage of the sales. Many times, we went to the beach with Cirilo, his wife, Isabel, and their son, Nani. My father was a hard-working person all of his life. He was able to retire at the age of seventy-three, but he was very active until his death at the age of seventy-eight, a year after his heart attack and surgery.

I have to tell you about something that happened at the Pueblo Nuevo house my parents rented a while after they got married, just a few blocks from my grandparents. When Marita, my older sister, was about three and a half and I was almost two years old, something happened. My mom was taking a shower, and we were playing outside the bathroom door. We heard the music of a "comparsa" (a type of group you might hear in New Orleans) passing by. Marita climbed on a chair and unlocked the front door. She took me by the hand, and we began dancing on the sidewalk to their music. My mother had heard Marita move the chair, and even though she had soap all over her body, she put a dress on, ran out of the house, and found us walking down the sidewalk, dancing with the music. That was enough for my parents to decide to move to La Playa, where my mother's family lived. There, she had the help and support of her family, especially my grandmother Aurora (Mamama).

We moved into my grandparents' compound and lived in the house addition my uncle built next to our grandparents' house. The main house was big, and in there lived my grandparents; Juan and Aurora; Aunt Marta and her brother Juanito (we called him Ino because he was Marita's godfather); Juanito's wife, Herminia (we called her Ina since she was Marita's godmother); and their children, Juanito (Chito) and José Antonio (Tatoño). Their third son, Alberto, had not been born yet. Ina was a great seamstress and made all of our beautiful dresses. The addition had a living room, a large bedroom, a kitchen with a dining area, and a bathroom. It was big enough for the four of us.

When my mom was getting ready to have Marita and me, she went to her parents' house to give birth there. In the end, four sisters and all of my cousins were born at my grandparents' home in La Playa, all with the help of the same midwife, named Panchita. This was a beach house in the suburb of La Playa, in the province of Matanzas, Cuba. We loved our time in that house, and I was surrounded by grandparents, aunts, an uncle, and cousins till I was eight years old. Then we moved to different places in the city until we left for the United States on June 22, 1971.

The small addition my Uncle Ino built next to my grandparents' beach house, which faced the Callejon de Jorge García in the front, was connected to my grandparents' house by an internal, cemented courtyard where all of the cousins played baseball, hopscotch, and softball. We also roller-skated and rode our scooters.

My grandfather Juan—we called him Papi—also owned the grocery store, which was on the corner next door to the main house. He owned that big corner until he sold the grocery store to a family that later became part of our family too. Behind the grocery store was an efficiency, which was connected to the store and had a small patio with a door to the large courtyard. My aunt Marta lived there after marrying the new store owner's older son at the age of fifteen. His name was Mario. He was twenty-one and was taking care of the store. Mario's parents lived on a farm in a town called Canasí, located on the outskirts of Matanzas.

This beach house was small, but it was enough for the four of us since my sister and I were toddlers. We enjoyed playing with our cousins and were always exhausted at the end of the day. Our parents always rocked us before we went to bed, listening to music on the radio. We were happy to have our grandmother Aurora there too. She was the one taking care of us when we were sick. We were very happy to have our family surrounding us. We could walk two blocks to the beach and enjoy the sea breeze.

The house also had a nice garden in the front, where we used to play and watch butterflies. A trellis went from one side of the front of the house to the back side of the other house, where Aunt Marta eventually lived, separating the front yard from the courtyard. My mother had the house decorated very simply. In the living room, she had her upright piano, with a crocheted tapestry she had made on top of it. There was a wooden living room set, with backs and seats made of cane, which consisted of a sofa, two rocking chairs, two armchairs, and a coffee table, plus an upright radio.

The living room had a door to the front garden and a window to the small courtyard. In the bedroom, she had her wooden bedroom set, which included a wardrobe (most of the old houses in Cuba do not have closets in their bedrooms, so you need wardrobes), a double bed for Marita and me to sleep in, and a crib for Margarita, who was born there later on. The bedroom had a window to the large yard, which was full of fruit trees that belonged to the house next to my grandparents'. I remember that we used to jump out of the bedroom window and into the next-door backyard to eat their mangos and guavas. The fruits tasted better when you picked them from the trees and ate them. The neighbors gave us permission to do that, and we surely enjoyed it. In the kitchen, she had a propane stove, a dining table with four chairs, and a nevera (an ice box). My father bought a refrigerator later on. The kitchen had a door to the courtyard. Next to the kitchen was the bathroom, which just had a shower, a sink, and a toilet. It also had a window to the courtyard.

We lived all together on the same corner where the grocery store and three living places were, all sharing the large interior courtyard. My mom and my aunt Herminia got pregnant almost at the same time. She had the boys, and my mom had the girls. Mamama made us lunch many times, and it usually consisted of a piece of Cuban bread with cooked olive oil and garlic spread on it. We also loved her yellow grits, mixed with a fried egg inside, and bananas. As a child living close to the beach, I remember waking up in the mornings and smelling the sea.

Here I am at four and a half years old, with a Shirley Temple hairstyle! It took my mom a while to get those curls into my hair, but they did not last long.

14

I hated my straight, reddish-auburn hair because the kids at the public school bullied me. The school was across the street from my grandparents', and it was where I completed first and second grade. Kids made fun of me and called me Prince Valiant, saying I looked like a roach because of the color of my hair. Because of this, my mother decided to curl my hair with a product called "Toni," but the curls did not last. When I was older, I was taken to a beauty parlor, and I had done what we called a "croquinole." My head was connected to this machine through hanging cables. It burned my hair somehow.

Chapter 2

Let me tell you about the González side of my family. My grandfather was Juan González Rodríguez. He was a politician and became Councilman in the city of Matanzas in the 30s. He had that position for eight years after his re-election. He tried again in 1957 and was elected, but he renounced his position after seeing all of the killings and the problems with the Batista dictatorship and the rebels.

His parents, Jose and Julia, were from Las Palmas in the Canary Islands, Spain. They had seven children, and because his father died when he was only seven years old, Papi had to help raise his younger brothers and work the farm. He was a very well-mannered man who never raised his voice. He always had something nice to say to his grandchildren. He was thin and short and had green eyes. That's how I remember him.

As a child, my grandfather had to quit school and help his mother by working the land in order to support the rest of the children. My grandfather educated himself by reading books. He always told us, "Instruction is what you acquire in school, but education is what you are born with and what is instilled into you by your family." He played the guitar and could improvise songs while singing Cuban country music. He smoked too much, and even though he quit for years, he eventually died at the age of sixty-five from emphysema. He was a sweet grandpa, and we miss him dearly. Papi was the patriarch of the family, and my grandmother Aurora Martínez Suárez was the matriarch until she died a few months before reaching one hundred years old. Both were Spaniard descendants from the Canary Islands, where Mamama was born.

Mamama's Martínez family came to Cuba but had to go back to where they were from—Las Palmas in the Canary Islands of Spain—during the Cuban-Spanish war in 1895. My great-grandparents got onto a ship with nine children. Someone got on board with black measles, and many children and some adults died from it. They lost their fourteen-year-old daughter, Margarita; a nine-year-old son; and another six-year-old girl. To prevent their bodies from being thrown overboard, the family acted as if they were sleeping, as they knew they were about to reach land. They were buried in Tenerife, the island before the one they were going to in the Canary Islands.

Mamama always told us that her mother suffered too much from the loss of her beautiful children, especially Margarita, but because of their action, at least they were buried instead of being thrown overboard, which was what happened to all of the other children and adults who died on the ship. What an awful thing for parents to go through!

My great-grandmother Francisca Suárez Suárez, who was married to Antonio Martínez Ojeda, had a total of twenty-one children! They were farmers. Their forty hectares of land were beautiful! The farm was called Finca El Sol. It had the Canímar River running through it, and it also had acres of beachfront. They lost a twenty-two-year-old son called Manuel in that river.

When the Cuban government wanted to build the Canímar bridge to make a shorter road to Varadero Beach, they had to ask her permission to build it, and my family approved it. When she passed away, she left that land (120 acres) to the nine children who were still alive. My grandmother Aurora's brothers and sisters could not get together and make the right decision about what to do with all that land after their mother passed away, so they sold it to a land developer for almost nothing and divided the money. Secundino, one of my mother's uncles, bought a car with some of that money, and his oldest and only son, Walberto, only nineteen years old, died in a car accident while driving it. I remember how hard it was for my mother when she heard the news of her first cousin's death, and her uncle was so distraught that he almost lost his mind.

My grandmother Aurora was born in Las Palmas of the Canary Islands in Spain. Her parents went back to Cuba when she was only three years old. As an adult, she had healing powers and was able to communicate with the dead. She was considered a doctor because of all of the ways she knew to make people better by using medicinal plants. Many people in the neighborhood came to see her when a child or someone in their family was sick and they could not afford to take them to a doctor. It was kind of scary for the young ones to see her in a trance, but to the rest, she was someone they could go to for a consultation about life and the future. I believe she was a spiritualist. When we got a cold or had a stomach problem, my grandmother came and used old remedies to cure us. She lived to be almost one hundred years old!

Thank God I do not have those powers, but my mother did, and thank God she did not use them the same way Mamama did. Years later, in the United States, Mom became part of a charismatic group at a Catholic church. She had healing hands. My mom was considered a prophet until the day she died. Some members of the church came and brought her communion every week when she was sick. Mima, even though she was a piano and kindergarten teacher, never taught in a school because my father wanted her at home taking care of us. She played all children's songs, and we sang along. She surely knew how to entertain us!

Aunt Marta was only seven years old when my sister Marita was born, so she is like another sister to us, and that is the way it still is today. Marta got married too young, and Mayito, her only child, was born when she was sixteen. He grew up at the beach house and is like another brother to us. He was born before my sister Julita. Aunt Marta got divorced later on, then went to school and got her teaching degree. She was a beautiful young woman who dedicated her life to her son. She taught many years in Cuba, and when she came to the United States, she went back to school, got her bachelor's degree, and taught until she retired. She did not remarry again until she was sixty-three. She married Miguel, a widower from Holguin, Oriente. On January 31ˢt, 2007, they moved to Puerto Rico, where Mayito was living. He had a car financing business there. They still live on Luquillo Beach in Puerto Rico.

In those years, the majority of women did not work outside of their homes. They were in charge of being housewives, cleaning, cooking, and taking care of their children while their husbands worked. That was the way it was in my family too. I remember my mother, aunts, and grandmother taking a break after lunch to listen to soap operas on the radio while sewing, knitting, and embroidering.

Someone very dear to me was my godmother, Celina. She was my mom's first cousin, and my godfather was her father, Eusebio, my mom's uncle from her father's side. They lived in the beach neighborhood, close to our home. She had a younger brother named Carlos, who was about ten years older than I was, and she started taking care of him when he was only one year old, when their young mother passed away from a bad case of measles. Madrina—that was what I called her—was only sixteen, and she had to raise her brother, cook for her father, and do all of the house chores. Tío Eusebio never got married again.

Madrina Celina was single and used to bring me over to her house to spend weekends with them. Her father's brother, named Tío Cheo, was married to her mother's cousin—whom they called Tía Luisa—and lived next door. Luisa was going through nervous breakdowns. It seemed that she had mental problems, but I don't know what type. They had four teenage children: Maria, Luis, Orlando, and Fernando. Both houses connected to each other by a door in their living rooms, and they also shared the front porch. One morning when I was staying there, we heard screaming coming from next door. We ran into the living room, and Madrina opened the door. I saw that in the middle of their living room, hanging from the central beam, was Tía Luisa. She had committed suicide. It was a horrible view, one that I have never forgotten.

Later in life, my uncle Ino and his family moved to a house he built in the community of San Rafael in Pueblo Nuevo, and my grandparents, along with Aunt Marta and Mayito, bought a house near my uncle not too long after. The beach house was left empty, and Papi rented it to his brother Tío Cheo and his new wife, Tutu.

Many years later, after we were all gone from Cuba, we heard that Tío Cheo's oldest son, Fernando, committed suicide like his mother, Tía Luisa, had. I remember him being tall and good-looking, with dirty blond hair and green eyes. I heard that he did it because his only teenage daughter, who was also beautiful and had blond hair and green eyes, ran away from home with a guy. He could not deal with what his daughter had done. She was his doll! He followed in his mother's steps by committing suicide!

Another awful thing that happened to Madrina was that her brother Carlos—a tall, handsome twenty-four-year-old with dirty blond hair and green eyes—who had just gotten married, had an accident while riding in a government jeep after joining Castro's forces, and he was left paralyzed from the waist down. His father, Eusebio, was upset about this horrible situation, and one night after work, he walked to the beach. Madrina told her father's brother Tio Cheo that he was not home yet and that she was worried. The next day, he was found lying face down by the beach shore. It seemed he had been taking some medications, which caused him to faint, fall face down in the water, and drown.

As a child, I remember asking Cousin Carlos why he was marrying his ugly girlfriend, because to me, she was ugly. She had a face full of pimples and a long nose, and she was as skinny as a rail. His answer was that her beauty was on the inside, not the outside. At the time of the accident, she was pregnant, and months later she had a son who looked just like his father. After his accident, and when their son was about two years old, Carlos noticed that his wife had eyes for a guy who was working with her. He could not tolerate her being unfaithful to him; therefore, he divorced her.

Unfortunately, that's how she showed her inside beauty! Carlos moved in with his father and sister. When she took off, she left the little boy for Madrina to take care of, as the boy did not want to leave his father's side. He disliked the man his mother had married and did not want to look at his baby sister. That poor child lived through many traumatic experiences in life! Finally, he moved back with his mother.

Years passed. Carlos and Madrina moved to Varadero Beach. By then, I was in the forced mobile labor camp unit, planting pine trees to make a wind curtain in the area of Punta Hicacos, north of Varadero Beach. I asked Madrina if I could stay with her and Carlos so I did not have to wake up early in the morning and travel that far every day. Madrina accepted, and after less than a week, she told me I had to leave her house because my presence at their place was affecting Carlos's position with the Revolution. People in the government were asking him how he could have someone who was against Castro's regime in his house. I left crying, feeling so hurt and unwanted, but at the same time, I understood the situation I had put him in with my presence.

Carlos was with the communist government. He was even sent to Czechoslovakia after his accident to see if they could improve his paralysis so he would be able to continue working for the Revolution. The only thing that it improved was his incontinence. I was bringing Carlos trouble and conflict with the government because of my presence! I forgave them for what they had to do. That was the last time I saw them.

Unfortunately, Carlos died at the age of thirty-eight from pernicious anemia. We were living in Miami when we heard the news. He was too young to die, and the only consolation was that his miserable life was over. Madrina, his sister, had dedicated her life to taking care of him until his death. He was really like a son to her, as she had raised him from infancy. After his death, Madrina moved back to her house in Matanzas, met someone, and got married. Years later, they got divorced. The family felt that he married her just for the house she had, which was a lot according to Cuban standards. She died in her seventies. I heard that she was placed in a mental hospital by her nephew because she was constantly praying on her knees. She lived a life full of suffering, but she faced everything with endurance.

Chapter

3

I have to tell you about my other side of the family. For years, we were the only grandkids in my father's family. Abuela Zoila Verrier Barnet and Abuelo Antonio Barnet Herrera were first cousins. Abuela's family was French, and they came to Cuba in 1803. There were twelve farms that belonged to French families, and they were located in Las Piedras in the province of Matanzas. Three of them belonged to Verrier families. We imagine that all of these Verriers were related, because all of these farms were located in the same area. It seems that Jules, our great-great-grandfather, was the last one from those three families who came to Cuba.

The Verriers were dedicated to education. One of my great-grandaunts, Ruperta Verrier, was also a school principal like my great-grandmother. Above are pictures of my grandparents Antonio and Zoila at a young age. We grew up visiting our great-grandmother, who lived to be ninety years old. She suffered through the death of two of her children, Mariano and our grand-mother Zoila.

The Barnet family went from England to Cataluña in Spain, and from there they emigrated to Cuba. Our great-granduncle José Agripino Barnet was born in Barcelona, Spain, on June 23, 1864. He was Consul of Cuba from 1902-1908 in Paris, France, and other countries, and then he became Cuba's Secretary of State. He later became interim President of the Republic of Cuba from 1935-36, right before the elections. Another great-granduncle Dr. Joaquín Buenaventura Barnet was a scientist who collaborated with Dr. Carlos J. Finlay in the discovery of the yellow fever. He died in the US while working on finding the cure to tuberculosis, a sickness he contracted and died from. These two families were very distinguished and well educated.

Irma and Mirta Barnet Verrier, our aunts, adored us. They had beautiful blue eyes like our great-grandmother María Néstora Barnet. My father and Tío Gonzalo had hazel eyes. They all showered us with love and affection. My aunts were always picking Marita and me up and taking us to our grandparents' home to spend weekends with them, and this gave my mother a break. We were like their daughters. Tío Gonzalo Barnet was the youngest one, and he studied telegraphy but never worked in this field. He died from emphysema at the age of sixty-five. Marita and I were the ones they spoiled the most because the other ones were smaller.

I adored my aunts! Irma was always contacting me, until the time of her death at the age of seventy-eight. She died from breast cancer. Aunt Irma was a teacher, and she also graduated from the University of Havana with a degree in pedagogy. In Cuba, she worked as a teacher first, then became a school principal before she left the country.

24

Irma married Julio, and they had two children who were born in Cuba. Their names are Julio Antonio and Zoila María. Zoila has beautiful blue eyes, and Julio has green eyes. They came to the USA in 1969 as young children, and they grew up in Union City, New Jersey. Zoila does not remember

anything about Cuba, because she was only a toddler when she came. Julio remembers some because he was six years old. They were able to leave because Julio's brother and sister claimed them. Julio married Ania, and they have a daughter named Inez. Zoila married Richard, and they do not have any children.

Here are Abuelo and Tío Gonzalo with Aunt Irma and her family a few months before they left for the USA.

My aunt Mirta was the sweetest! After their mother, my abuela, passed away, she was in charge of the house chores. She married Miguel Angel and had two children: Miguel Angel Jr. and Justo Antonio. We do not think our grandfather ever had any intention of leaving the country, but he wanted to see the family together again. Maybe he was old and sick and thought he already had his home there. After Irma left the country, Mirta and her family moved into our grandfather's house. Tío Gonzalo lived there with them too. A few years after my grandfather retired, he had a stroke, which affected one side of his body. After we left the country, he had another stroke, and this time it was worse. He died a few years later.

Tío Gonzalo, Mirta, Miguel, and their sons, twelve and ten years old, finally left Cuba on May 13, 1980, during the **Mariel boat-**

lift. My father got a boat and picked them up. They were placed in another boat, not my father's. How were they able to come?

Let me give you some Cuban history. In April of 1980, a group of five Cubans drove a bus into the Peruvian Embassy in Havana. Cuban guards opened fire, and one of the soldiers died in the cross-fire. The government wanted the Peruvian government to release those five individuals and accused them of causing the death of the soldiers. The Peruvian government denied their release, and then the Cuban government withdrew the guards from their embassy.

Because of that, on Easter Sunday, about ten thousand Cuban citizens jumped the fence and crowded the place. People were even seated on trees branches because all of the space was taken. Then Fidel Castro announced that whoever wanted to leave could do so as long as they had someone from Miami to pick them up at the port of Mariel. This was the cause of the Mariel boatlift in 1980. Around 125,000 Cubans arrived in Florida. It was stopped by the United States when Castro emptied his jail cells and mental institutions and sent them to Florida.

My father, Chito, Rolando, and others chartered motor vessels and went to Cuba to pick up their families. Some of them could not bring anyone because their families were afraid of acts of repudiation that were taking place against those who were leaving. I will tell you about it later.

Aunt Mirta and her husband Miguel moved to Boston, where her husband's family was living. Their oldest son, Miguel Angel Jr., married a young lady from Venezuela. Her name is Antonieta, and they have

three children: Marianne, Miguel Angel III, and Marco Antonio. Their son Justo Antonio married a young lady from Nicaragua named Jhovanella, and they have two children: Antonio Lorenzo and Leonardo Angel. Miguel and Justo became great, hard-working men, and Miguel Angel Jr. even joined the US Army. Miguel Senior died at the age of seventy-seven, and our dear aunt Mirta died from complications from her rheumatoid arthritis at the age of seventy-nine.

In Cuba, Fidel Castro also ordered the elimination of all religious celebrations in 1969; therefore, Christmas wasn't allowed for almost thirty years. Our cousins Miguel A. Jr. and Justo Antonio did not know about Christmas. Justo was telling me that the first time he celebrated Christmas was when he was eleven years old, in 1980, when he came to the United States of America. He remembers that this moment was a special time in his life. It was something he had never experienced before, and the happiness of seeing a Christmas trees, the decorations, and all of those gifts was unbelievable. Here is Justo opening a gift during his first Christmas celebration at their father's family house in Boston.

Chapter
4

I will never forget the years we lived in La Playa. We had a lot of freedom and enjoyed a lot of outdoor activities. I remember that my mom got us ready every morning around 10:00 a.m. so we could walk to the beach with Aunt Ina and our two cousins "Chito" and "Tatoño", who were the same ages as us, just a few days apart. Cousin Alberto was born, and after that Ina lost her fourth child, a baby girl, when she was eight months pregnant. The family was devastated, especially Ina!

We enjoyed playing in our grandparents' courtyard, but we also loved holding on to our cousins' bikes while riding our roller-skates on the deserted streets. We often collected flowers in the empty field across the street, and later on we played in the houses that they were building there. We also sang and played on my grandparents' house's front porch, even at night, as it had a long fluorescent light that was always lit. We had so much enjoyment, and we felt safe. Our parents kept watching us, and our mothers kept calling our names to find out where we were. If we were playing hide and seek, we never answered to them, as we did not want to be discovered.

One time, when houses across the street were being built, all of the cousins went into one of the houses out of curiosity. Our cousin Alberto, who was three years old then, was with us too. We were just roaming around the house when we suddenly heard a loud bump. Albert had fallen into the house's septic tank! Those houses in that area had septic tanks instead of the sewer. Thank God there was a little bit of water inside the tank to break the fall, but the water level was not over his head. Chito ran to let our mothers know what had happened so they could help us get him out of there. Alberto was fine, but we were all scared. Our mothers were upset and very mad at us. We were all punished for going inside those houses.

In those years, my father got an offer from a big clothing material distributor in Havana, which made him decide to leave the store where he had been working for years. This company gave my father a two-seater car, which we called "La Cuña," the Wedge. Two years later, when he went back to work for Cirilo, the owner of La Casa Verde, because he made him an offer he could not refuse, he bought a car. This car was bigger and better. I do not remember which type he bought, though. In the evenings, we used to get in this car, and my father would drive all the way down to Canímar. I loved when he drove by the seawall and we got to see the city lights reflected on the water of Matanzas Bay, the car windows open, letting the breeze pass through. We listened to soft American music that my dad was able to find on the car radio.

We did not have a television set at home then, but my father bought a radio, so he was able to listen to stations from different countries. He especially liked the baseball games. I did not enjoy spending beautiful Sundays listening to those games. He did not want to take us to the beach then, as he did not want to miss the baseball game. And besides that, that was the only day he was at home. I still hate when my husband, Bob, spends beautiful Sundays watching games. I just get my purse and go shopping!

The beach near our home was at Matanzas Bay, and it was beautiful. Its water was like glass. It was called La Playita de los Pinos (Pine Beach) because it had a lot of pine trees. I heard it does not exist anymore. The Castro government built a road going through it. We, and other kids in the neighborhood, played in the sand and water under the surveillance of our mothers while our dads were working.

Summer vacations were the best since we were able to go to the beach every morning. We got very tanned because we did not have any sunblock lotion. As a matter of fact, when we were teenagers, we used baby oil with iodine as a bronzer. We got beautiful tans and wore light colored dresses, showing our shoulders so others could see them. Our hair got lighter too. That was the summer look! By the way, in Cuba you can go to the beach during the entire year because winters are mild.

There was an-
other beach about
twenty minutes away,
which we used to go
to on the weekends.
Its name is Bueyva-
quita. This picture of
Margarita, Marita,
Julita and me was
taken there. Back then, they had rental cabins so you could change and keep your clothes in there. It had restrooms and a tiki bar cafeteria. It was a beach among the rocks, and the bay view was great. It was in an area that I believe belonged to a family who had a small building that looked like a castle and a house nearby. We spent the entire day there and purchased lunch at their cafeteria.

As teenagers, we had to go by bus or get a ride, as it was a long distance from where we lived then. We enjoyed that beach until it was expropriated by the government, and then things were not the same anymore. The cafeteria was closed!

The family who owned the castle had left for the USA, but one of the brothers, the youngest one, had to stay behind. It was big news when this young man was killed in a car/truck accident along with his eight-months-pregnant wife. I believe they left behind a smaller daughter. We saw the wreck. It happened in front of the cathedral. It was awful. Years later, the other brother, an architect, made my sister Mirtica's house plans for her beautiful, three-story Florida Keys house.

By the time I began kindergarten at St. Vincent de Paul Catholic School, our sister Margarita had already been born. My mom had been pregnant between us, but she fell down while hanging clothes on the line and miscarried another girl. My father was always blaming my mother for having only girls, till her gynecologist told him that the man was the one who determined the baby's sex. That doctor was taking care of her during her last pregnancy. After that, my dad shut his mouth and never complained again. By the end of his life, he let us know how happy he was that he had only girls. He was glad we stayed by him until his time of death.

I remember our mother, Mima, being thin and beautiful when I was a child. Her hair was brown and wavy, and she had big brown eyes. She had beautiful hands that did not show any arthritis, even at the end of her life. In the afternoons, before having us take a nap, she would play the piano, and we all sang. While we were sleeping, she did the laundry by hand and ironed. Even the sheets and my father's underwear were ironed with some starch. She was always a busy mom. She had a great smile, as she had beautiful teeth that she took great care of her whole life.

Mima helped Tía Ina decorate our dresses with ribbons and lace, and she also was good at doing embroidery work. Marita and I sometimes wore matching dresses and matching bows in our hair. My mom had the girls, and Aunt Ina had the boys. My sister Marita and I shared a double bed, which was great in winter because it was cold. We slept back to back! We are sixteen months apart.

Below is my mom; our aunts Mirta, Marta, and Irma; and me, Margarita, and Marita. You can see the upright piano in the background.

When I was almost five, a horrible hurricane passed by and devastated the beach area. Everybody listened to what my grandfather had to say and did it. He did not want us to leave the beach house, because he thought it was safe. We all stayed, and those were awful and scary hours that we endured! Before the wind got stronger, soldiers passed by asking everybody to evacuate the beach because they thought a tsunami was coming, but my grandfather and other families did not listen to them. I learned that life is more important than material things. When they tell you to evacuate, leave, especially near the beach.

We were all bundled together in a bedroom next to the living room, all of the kids and mothers in bed. The wind got worse, and people closer to the beach came over seeking refuge in our house because the winds destroyed theirs. Our grandparents' house was full of people! I remember women praying and children crying, and I saw a group of men trying to hold the front door to keep it closed.

The next day, our house, the addition my uncle built, had lost its roof. When we got there, I saw that the piano was all wet. My father was selling jewelry as a part-time job. Thank God that all of the jewelry was still in the wardrobe and did not get lost. Some got wet, but not the watches. It was a big mess! We all ended up having to stay in my grandparents' house until the roof was repaired. It was crowded in there!

As I got older, I realized that the area we lived in as small children was a great place for children to grow up in, especially because it puts them in touch with nature. They have the freedom to play outside with their friends, be around nature, learn about animals and vegetation, and, the most precious thing, be close to the beach and enjoy it.

Children who grow up in the city are limited to the inside of their homes. Perhaps once in a while, their families take them to the park. Their learning environment is more limited and in less contact with nature. At least our children grew up in a small community and were able to play outside with their friends, as there was not much traffic. Later on, we bought a five-acre farm not too far from the city, and there they played outside most of the time and enjoyed it. But when they got older and wanted to go to parties, they questioned why we moved so far from everybody. Now you have the answer, Bobby and Marc!

Chapter

5

For my sixth birthday, my grandmother Zoila gave me a beautiful watch. It had a yellowish face. I am wearing it in this picture. I thought it was dirty, because I had never seen a watch with a face that color. Then I decided to wash it, not realizing that I was just ruining it. My grandmother got mad at me, and I was upset that I broke my new watch. My sister Marita got one too, but hers had a different face color. It was white!

My grandmother had inherited those watches from her mother, and then my aunts had them, and she saved them for her

granddaughters, so they were really antique. You cannot imagine how I felt when I saw my grandmother's face. She was trying to hide how upset she was, but I could tell. I cried because of what I had done. I felt guilty and could not fix it.

Thinking back now, I feel that the adults should have explained to me that even though the face of my watch was yellowish, that was the way it was supposed to be. They knew I was concerned about it.

Marita and Margarita have beautiful features like my mother's. I look more like my father, but with brown eyes. We all have my mother's brown eyes, which are like our grandmother's. We did not get the blue and green eyes from my father's side. In those years, the Shirley Temple look was fashionable, and all of the mothers tried to give their daughters that look. Many of our dresses, especially the ones we were wearing in the birthday pictures, were made by Aunt Ina and my mom. They were made of taffeta, which was also fashionable then.

Marita and I began attending St. Vincent de Paul Catholic School, which was the private school that our mother graduated from and had her wedding at. She always wanted us to go to her school. I was in kindergarten, and Marita first grade. One day, I fell down during recess and broke my elbow. The nuns did not call my father to let him know what had happened to me. My parents were very upset at the nuns because they had let me spend the entire day in pain, with an inflamed arm, and had not notified my father. When I got home at 6:00 p.m., my parents took me to the emergency room. At the emergency room, Dr. Murphy put my elbow back in place without anesthesia. That was so painful that I wet my pants. Because of this, right away, our parents signed us up for La Virgen Milagrosa Catholic School, but they had a long waiting list. For the time being, we were sent to the public school Escuela Pública #18, just a few steps from our home.

The day of my party. In the front row, from left to right, are: first cousins Alberto and Juan (Chito), second cousins Lilia and Marta, my sister Marita, me (Nery), my sister Margarita, and my second cousin Ramirito. Behind him is my first cousin José Antonio (Tatoño), and next to him is my second cousin Tony. Behind the sofa are my friends. From the left: Alejandrina, Graciela, Berta, Filiberto, and Panchito. In the back row: Tía Mirta, my second cousin Mercedes, a friend Benigno, my second cousin Blanca, and Tía Marta and her friend Marta.

It was easier for my mom to just walk us there and pick us up after school. All of my first and second cousins were at that school too! Every morning when we got to the new school, they gave us milk with powdered wheat (gofio) inside, even though we had already had breakfast at home. But I sure loved the smell and taste of that cup of milk!

Everybody there knew my family, as my grandfather's grocery store was across the street. It was a nice, mixed school, and that was what my father did not want for us. He wanted us to go to an all-girls Catholic private school. I just think that it would have been more fun to be in a mixed school, especially the one a few steps from home, but they wanted us to have a good Catholic education.

The picture below was taken during a show at Escuela Pública #18. My cousin Marta is standing in the middle. She has bows in her beautiful curls. Sitting down to the left is my cousin Lilia, also with Shirley Temple curls. This was the pre-kindergarten class. I am the one with the umbrella. I have straight hair. Kids called me Prince Valiant, and later on they called me Christopher Columbus! By then, Tío Fulgencio, Marta and Lilia's grandfather, had built three houses for him and his sons in a neighborhood called Naranjal, and their families moved away from La Playa neighborhood.

Chapter

6

By the time we were accepted at La Virgen Milagrosa Catholic School, I was in third grade, so of course, we—especially me—were missing the fun of a mixed school. I was seven years old. Marita was placed in fourth grade. That year, Marita got sick with hepatitis and could not go to school for about four months. I tried to help her do homework and read her grade books. When she went back to school, the school principal, Sister (Sor) Carmen, began asking her verbally about different areas of study. I was there with them and helped her with some of the answers. She began asking me questions too and realized that I knew all of the answers. It was then when I was placed a year ahead of my grade; therefore, I ended up in the same class as my sister.

La Virgen Milagrosa school was nice, but the nuns were very strict, and right after lunchtime, we had to do embroidery work and say the rosary. You were not allowed to talk until classes began in the afternoon at 2:00 p.m. The school was also a convent, and the majority of the nuns were young. One of them was young and beautiful. Her name was Sister (Sor) Maria. When the nuns were sent into exile after the government private schools' expropriation, Sister Maria met someone in the USA and got married. We learned to like the nuns, and we received an excellent education. We took English as a second language, and since the groups were smaller, we had a lot of attention. This is my first school picture at the new school.

When Marita and I were attending school, the bus picked us up at the beach house early in the mornings and took us there. After doing our homework, we went roller-skating, holding on to our cousins' bikes or to the bumpers of cars when they left my grandfather's store parking space. I am telling you, we had great guardian angels! The first three girls never had a bike, but the last two did because I bought each of them one when I began working as a teenager. Everything changed when we moved to the city. We could not play in the streets or enjoy our cousins like we were used to. It was very boring, and we could not wait to visit them.

At school, we made new friends, including the twins María Rosa and Hilda Rosa, whose father had a shoe store next to La Casa Verde; Sarita, whose aunt lived next to us when we lived on America Street; María de los Angeles, whose father had a movie theatre; María Luisa and Lourdes, whose father was a doctor in town; and many others.

On Sundays, the school bus picked us up to take us to the school church, and in the afternoons all of the cousins and some friends would gather in my grandparents' living room to watch movies and programs on TV like *The Lone Ranger*, Laurel and Hardy shows, and *Lassie*. It was a lot of fun growing up with the whole family. Our grandparents were glad to have all of their grandchildren in their living room, enjoying the afternoon and having lemonade Mamama made for all of us.

The school had a nice percussion band, and I played the tambor. I loved to participate in parades, and I remember Sister Maria walking next to us, men whistling at her when she passed by. She was so attractive that men could not control themselves! I could not believe what was happening! We learned different folklore dances, and we were part of the school church choir. We were always very active in all of the activities available to us.

Three of my sisters took communion at La Virgen Milagrosa Chapel. It was the beautiful chapel where we attended mass every Sunday. I loved the month of May because every Friday we offered flowers to Virgin Mary and sang. Some girls were chosen to be dressed like angels during this special ceremony. We were also part of the school choir. That's the month when girls took their first communion too.

At this ceremony, a girl dressed like an angel was assigned to each girl receiving the sacrament. Marita had her communion at St. Vincent de Paul and had no angel next to her, but she was my angel at my communion. I was Margarita's, Margarita was Julita's and Julita was Mirtica's, but Mirtica could not have communion at the school chapel because it was destroyed by Castro's communist soldiers after it was confiscated. She had hers at the Carmelitas Church.

40

In those years, high school went up to eighth grade. I was very well developed, and when I was in eighth grade, one of the priests was always putting one of his arms around my shoulder, reaching to touch my breast. It felt so uncomfortable that I mentioned it to my mother. She told me not to say anything to my father, as she was afraid of his reaction. She decided instead to come with me to school and speak to the school principal. At the time, that was Sor Engracia, a Spanish nun.

When my mother told Sor Engracia that Father Vila was always trying to touch my breasts, she was furious. She could not believe I was accusing Fr. Vila of something that low! She began defending him, mentioning all of his good deeds and what a dedicated man of God he was. She then stood up and called me a liar. She began asking me how I could say something like that about a man who was like a saint. My mouth and eyes were wide open because I could not believe how blinded she was. My mother was astonished, paralyzed with anger because of the unbelievable attitude of this nun. My mom then stood up and grabbed me by the hand, and we left. On the way home, my mom told me that since it was my last year there, every time I saw that priest, I needed to walk away from him. It was really a shocking experience, one that I have never forgotten, because I was telling the truth and could not believe this nun would not believe me, instead calling me a liar and insulting me and my mother. It was very disenchanting!

I learned to love and respect all of them. I was one of their best students there, always achieving high marks. Even though I felt hurt by her accusations, her and the priest's actions did not kill my faith in God. On the contrary, it grew deeper, and I prayed harder for them to be forgiven. They are human beings, and they made mistakes. This was a tremendous mistake the nun was making, as that priest was a child molester. She did not want to admit it.

Below, I am pictured with my classmates, my sister Marita, Sor Engracia, Sor Maria, and one of our teachers.

When we moved to the Río #42 altos house, my younger sisters did not need to ride the bus anymore to go to La Virgen Milagrosa, and my dad walked them to school. They liked it much better. But when all of the private schools were confiscated, they were sent to a public school less than a block from our home. What a big, awful change that was for them!

Chapter

7

My uncle Juan had a construction company that was growing nicely, bringing him a good amount of capital. He had several trucks and a barge. He began building a chalet in a new neighborhood located in Pueblo Nuevo, called Reparto San Rafael. The house had granite flooring, with his initials printed in it on the front porch. It had a living room, a kitchen with a dining area, three bedrooms, a bathroom, and a carport that had a cement sink for the laundry. The front garden had the type of grass you do not have to cut, and there were fruit trees planted in the backyard.

My grandparents bought a house in Pueblo Nuevo, and a few months later my grandfather passed away at sixty-five from emphysema. My grandmother and Aunt Marta eventually sold that house and bought a chalet in the same neighborhood as my uncle, two blocks away from where my uncle's chalet was. Later on, the communist government built ugly rectangular buildings in this beautiful neighborhood, which ruined the picturesque community.

Years later, when my husband and I traveled to Europe and visited countries that were previously communist, the same thing had been done to many of their nice communities. One that caught our attention was in Tallin, Estonia. Some of those buildings were going to be demolished in order to preserve this particular, beautiful construction style in this particular community. Good for them!

All of us together at my grandmother's carport in Reparto San Rafael. Marita was engaged to Rolando, and Chito was engaged to Magaly.

From left to right, standing: Tatoño; Chito; his wife, Magaly; Ina; Ino; Mamama; Marta; Mario; his parents, Maria and Julian; me (Nery); Marita; her husband, Roly; Mima; and Pipo.

Seated: Margarita, Mirtica, Julita, Mayito, Alberto, and Mayito's friend. This picture was taken after Papi passed away, and Mamama and Marta purchased this house to be closer to my uncle Ino.

My first cousin Chito was able to leave Cuba in 1970 by going through Mexico, leaving his wife, Magaly, and his children, Juan Carlos and Lizbet, behind. They had another son, named Danny, who was born in the USA. Magaly and their children were able to leave in 1971 via Spain and joined him in New Jersey in 1972, where he was living. Chito and Magaly spent more than a year in forced labor camps. His brother Tatoño and his wife, Idoris, were able to come to the USA in 1995 on a visitor's visa. He was fifty-two years old. Their daughters, Liliana and Neyda, eventually joined them.

In 1999, Alberto, their younger brother, was finally allowed to go to Canada with his wife, Aidita, to visit their daughter Yanet, her husband, Oviel, and their children, who were living there already. The second time that Alberto and Aidita were allowed to go to Canada, they crossed the bridge to the American side and were admitted into the USA. They were accepted by the USA because the country's law at that time—Wet Foot, Dry Foot, which was for Cuban refugees seeking freedom—allowed them to stay.

Alberto was so happy to finally be free but was worried about Mariela, his younger daughter, who was left behind in Cuba with her husband. Unfortunately, three months after arriving in the United States in 2002, he died of a heart attack. This was very painful for the entire family, especially for his father, who had come to America a few years earlier with Tía Herminia, and she passed away not too long after achieving freedom, as well. It was very unfortunate for all of them, and for our entire family. Alberto had his youngest daughter still in Cuba, whom he was trying to get out as soon as he came here. She finally was allowed to leave Cuba, and her husband joined her later on. His family is all together now, enjoying freedom. Ino, their father, died years later at the age of ninety-two.

Our second cousins Lilia, Maria Elena, Marta, Luisito, and Tony, along with their families, were not able to leave Cuba, and they stayed there, enduring the communist dictatorship. It was very rough for them, as they did not believe in that system. For whatever reason, they could not leave even though their grandmother Tía Maria was a Spaniard. They could not take her Spanish citizenship because, for years, only sons and daughters could.

Their grandfather, who was my grandmother Aurora's brother, Tío Fulgencio, was born in Cuba, but as a child he went with his parents on a ship to the Canary Islands during the Spanish-American War. They had to leave Cuba because were afraid for their lives. That was the reason my grandmother was born in Spain. Another second cousin named Ramirito was able to leave after spending some time in jail as a political prisoner. He was caught when trying to leave the island by boat. Mamama and Mima visited Cuba in 1979. Mamama was eighty years old and wanted to see her only son in case something happened to her.

From my father's side, my first cousins Miguel Angel and Justo Antonio were able to come to the USA with Tía Mirta; their father, Miguel; and Tío Gonzalo when my father went to pick them up during the Mariel boatlift in 1980. Remember, I mentioned this before. My father, Chito, and others paid a shrimp boat to go to Cuba to pick their families up.

Instead of letting my father's family come with him, the government put them in a big boat with a bunch of weirdos. In my father's boat, they placed a bunch of men who were out of jail. Thank God they were able to come. They moved to Boston, where Miguel's family was living.

It was very emotional when my Aunt Mirta and I embraced after nine years of being away from each other. They did not spend too much time in Key West, but they were exhausted from their odyssey at sea, still wearing the same clothes they'd been wearing since the day they left Cuba.

When the officers got to their house to inform them that it was time for them to leave, as there was a boat waiting for them, they did not have time to pack anything, and the house was left with everything inside. The officers took them to the port of Mariel and put them on a boat. They were thrilled to finally to be able to leave!

When Fidel Castro saw that thousands of people wanted to leave the island, he put the jailed criminals in those boats, along with people from mental hospitals and people with tuberculosis and leprosy. Chito came back empty-handed because his father and brothers were afraid of the reprisals people were receiving when they tried to leave their homes to go to Mariel.

Many got scared to come because government thugs were attacking those who wanted to leave. One of our friends, Luisito, was tied to a car and pulled through the streets, and people threw things at him until he was so badly hurt that he needed hospitalization. He could not leave on the boat that came to pick him up. Years later, he was able to come, but he continued having health problems due to all of the internal injuries he suffered, and he eventually died.

Chapter 8

elow is a picture of my father at the store. He was so young
and had the big responsibility of supporting a wife and,
eventually, five daughters. He was a hard-working man
who always provided for his family. He worked until he was seventy-three and died five years later, when he was seventy-eight, after
having an open-heart surgery to replace his aorta valve and then
two bypasses. He lasted a year after this surgery, in and out of the
hospital until his body could not take it anymore.

As a Spanish descendant, my dad was admitted as a member of
the Casino Español, where great parties were offered for the members and their families. Remember that our ancestors came from
Barcelona and the Canary Islands.

Later on, my parents became members of the tennis club in the late fifties. It was a nice, modern club located in Peñas Altas, on  the way to Varadero Beach. It had a beach that we enjoyed when we had the opportunity to go, even when we went by bus as teenagers with our friends. It was a very nice place among the rocks, right on the Matanzas Bay. We also enjoyed the parties they had for their associates. It was fun.

We used to go to there with my sisters and friends during vacation. It was so nice to enjoy such a nice place. One morning at its beach, we were all having fun, and my younger sisters, Julita and Mirtica, were jumping from the rocks into the water with their lifesaver rings, which were becoming too small for them. Mirtica jumped headfirst and was left with her feet in the air, upside down, unable to bring her head up. She was stuck in the lifesaver ring! I saw her kicking desperately, so I jumped in the water and rescued her. She was so scared. Thank God we were watching her. Another day, our friend Ada jumped in the water, and when she came out, one of her breasts was showing. We began pointing to her breast, but she thought we were meaning a shark or something, and then she finally realized her breast was out. That was so embarrassing for her, as she was in front of all of the guys, who were laughing. She did not want to come out of the water again!

Going back to early years, Margarita, my middle sister, was also born at the beach house. She was a beautiful child and had blond

hair and pretty features (pictured with our mother). But I do not remember when her birth took place at home, as I was only four years old, and I think they took us to my other grandparents' house. My mother miscarried another baby between Margarita and Julita while she was hanging clothes on a line. I remember when Julita was born. All of them were running around, bringing clean, warm water into the only large bedroom the house had. I could hear my mother pushing and hurting, and then I heard the baby crying. I was relieved too. My grandmother always assisted the midwife during the process. My father waited with us in the living room to hear the baby cry.

The beach house became too small for all of us after Julita was born. At that point, we moved to the city of Matanzas. Julita surprised us by walking when she was only nine months old! Poor Julita was not able to enjoy those mornings at the beach.

The fifth girl was born at the hospital because Mima was having some complications. Mirta Alicia (Mirtica) was born with her umbilical cord around her neck, so thank God she was born at the hospital, because Mima had to have a C-section in order to be able to save her. She also had her tubal ligation done then. No more girls!

We grew up to be very close to each other, and that is the way we still are today, thank God. I jokingly tell them that when we get older, we need to get a big house where all of us can live together and have someone serving us. Then we tell our aunt Marta that if she starts to be a pain in the neck, she is not going to be able to share this place with us. We laugh about it, but who knows! Time will tell.

The Barnet sisters made sure that all of our children grew up close to each other so we could keep the same closeness we had with our own cousins. This binding is so important in a family, and I feel it is what makes our family whole. I love my sisters dearly and know that we will suffer when one of us is gone. It was the same way with my mom and her brother and sister.

Aunt Marta always felt like she was our sister instead of an aunt, as she was closer to us in age than to her sister, and that is the way we all feel about her too. She was still a child when Marita was born. At this moment, the same closeness exists among our children. They are trying to continue the tradition of keeping the family together by having their children grow up close to each other.

Chapter 9

After my grandfather Juan sold the grocery store, he opened his own distribution business. He went from grocery store to grocery store distributing many things, from crackers to candies to cookies, etc. His business was called La Veguita. One day, he came to bring us a can of crackers and was talking to my mother in the kitchen, but he left his van running in the driveway, parked in front of the trellis. I was a very curious girl, so I jumped in the van and moved the shifter. The van lurched forward, knocking down the trellis.

Pictured below is the van and Ina, Chito, Mamama, Tatoño, Papi, and Alberto.

Thank God I was able to stop it right in front of the kitchen door, where Papi and my mother were talking. They were so upset and scared. Looking back now, I realize that it was grandpa's fault for leaving the van running with kids around. I learned my lesson.

Another day, when I was only six years old, my mother was busy in the bedroom, rocking Margarita, who was running a fever. I wanted to have merengue, which is similar to toasting marshmallows, but she told me to wait. I did not listen to her and went ahead and began making them with the white part of the egg. I then got the rever-bero (a small, portable alcohol stove) she had on the counter. I got the flame going and began roasting them. Suddenly, I ran out of alcohol.

When I went to put more alcohol in, I did not notice that there was a little flame in there. The bottle of alcohol caught on fire, and I began screaming. My mother came into the kitchen while I was holding the bottle that was on fire. She told me to throw it, and the inflamed alcohol got all over the dining room tablecloth, which caught fire. My grandmother came over when she heard my moth-er's screams. The two of them were able to stop the fire by throwing pails of water on the table. I had some burns on my hands, but thank God there were not many. Mamama prepared some cream with aloe to calm the pain of the burns. The tablecloth was ruined, but the table was okay. What a scary moment that was! My fin-gers were hurting because I burned some of them. I always have been the go-and-get-it type of person, and that was what I did, but I could've burned the house down.

We had a beautiful field across from our house, and we used to go there, pick flowers, and bring them home to our mothers. Soon, they began building new houses in the field, and we used to go in those houses and play hide and seek when the workers were not there.

Our next-door neighbor had a goat called Cuca. Cuca really smelled! Even today, when someone passes by me who has not washed his or her hair, I tell Bob that it smells as bad as the goat Cuca. I had a milk intolerance, and that was the milk my mom gave me as a child. I remember that the neighbors had a floor tile fac-tory behind their house, and they made beautiful decorative tiles.

Most of the houses in the neighborhood were wood houses, but the new houses that were built across the street were made of concrete blocks.

Many of our second cousins lived near the beach house. One day, Marta, whom we called Mami, was playing with me. She had beautiful, curly, blond hair and blue eyes. We were pretending to be beauticians. She combed my straight, auburn hair, and I decided to give her a haircut. Her hair was like Shirley Temple's, full of beautiful curls, but I left her with only the two front curls. When I showed my mom what a beautiful haircut I had given her, she began crying; ran into the living room, where I had cut her hair; and picked up all of those curls to saved them for her mother.

When her mother arrived and saw what I did to her daughter, she began screaming, and then we were all crying. I really thought it was not a big deal, but they were very upset about what I had done to my cousin's beautiful curls. They could not forgive me for a while, and even as an adult, they continue to remind me about it when they see me. I feel it was my mom's fault for leaving the scissors accessible to a child and for not watching what we were doing closely.

All of my second cousins from my mom's side were blond and had blue eyes. They were also my first cousins and the boys' first cousins, as Ino and Ina were first cousins. The school was right on the street corner, and all of the cousins started school almost at the same time, as we were almost the same age. We were very active in all of the school's activities, and I did very well and finished second grade.

Then my parents decided to send us to a Catholic, private, all-girls school called La Virgen Milagrosa, where I began third grade. The school bus came to pick us up. Marita and I were up very early in the mornings to wait for the bus and were the last ones to get home. Ramon was the driver, and his daughters attended there too. The school was nice, run by the charity nuns. The nuns also lived there, and girls from other cities stayed there during the week. I felt sorry for them because they were missing their families.

When I was eight years old, we moved to the center of the city of Matanzas and moved into a remodeled house on St. Isabel Street, closer to my dad's work. Four of us were born then, and Julita, the youngest one then, was only nine months old. The house had a living room, two bedrooms separated by a bathroom, a dining room, and a kitchen. Julita learned how to walk there before she was a year old. I remember us having the measles, and Julita turned the bidet faucet on and got the water all over her, the bathroom, and the hall. It had a wall separating the neighbor's patio. We did not have any privacy; you could hear everything that was going on next door, and they could hear us too. My father bought a TV and a nice refrigerator.

The only good thing about this place was that it was near the beautiful Watkins Park and was closer to downtown and the San Juan River nearby. There was a girl who lived one block from us and attended our school. Her name was Lilia. She used to come over to the house and play with us, or we would go across the street where this big lady called Gisela taught us how to play Scrabble.

Two houses from ours, there was another girl named Zulema.

Her father, Alejandro, was the province representative and traveled to the USA a lot. He brought her beautiful walking dolls from there, and many other interesting toys. We loved to go there to play! Her mother prepared a room for her to keep her toys in, and we used to spend hours playing with these great toys. She was the youngest daughter of this couple. Her other sisters were already engaged or married. It seemed that her mother had had her during her menopause. Her father was always traveling, and we did not see him much. Their house had the latest technology then, like a great TV, a toaster, and a washer. I guess he bought all of these things while traveling.

One year, we had a rainy season for more than twenty days, and San Juan River flooded. The water came to the corner of the street. People from the health department went from house to house to vaccinate everybody. We were vaccinated by our doctor.

My father kept looking and found another house on America Street. It was an older, bigger place, but it only had two large bedrooms, one bathroom, a living room, a family room, a dining room, and a kitchen. The houses in the city were deep, long row houses, one next to the other, and ours had a cemented patio going from the family room to the kitchen. The floor had beautiful Spanish tile, high beam ceilings, and a big window and double doors in the living room. By then, there were four girls. Julita was only a year old.

Mima got pregnant with Mirtica and was having some problems with her pregnancy. My father hired a Spanish lady named Felicia to cook. Another lady was helping my mother with the laundry once a week, and for cleaning, there was a black lady called Edelmira who helped her. My mother always had Spanish cooks because that was the food my father liked. But when we went over to Abuela Zoila's house, her style was more French than Spanish. She did not fry the sliced, ripe plantains; she grilled them with wine. Delicious! Her "café con leche" was not like Mamama's because she put a pinch of salt and two teaspoons of sugar in it, and it was awful. We did not like the salt in it.

My dad's birthday was in March, and Julita was born in March, two days after my father's birthday. After celebrating Julita's first birthday at this house with family and friends, my grandmother Zoila died two days later. She was only fifty years old, but she suffered from high blood pressure. My grandmother Zoila suffered a pulmonary thrombosis due to this and died. It was a very traumatic experience for my family. While she was dying, my aunt Irma had to leave the house to find the doctor, but when she came back with him, my grandmother had already died in my aunt Mirta's arms from asphyxiation. They did not have a telephone at home.

My grandfather was not there, either, since he was already at work. He was the chief of the railroad station and always left very early in the morning. Finally, Irma was able to go next door to call my father, and when he got there, he found his mother dead on her bed, surrounded by my aunts and grandfather. My uncle Gonzalo was hospitalized at that moment, and my grandfather did not tell him about her passing until later. When he came back home from the hospital, he was looking for his mother and was devastated when he found out the news.

The family was overwhelmed with the news of her passing. Our abuela Zoila was very dear to us. She was the one who taught us how to play different board games and who always made special meals for us. Remember, we were the only grandkids in their family, and they showered us with love and attention.

Abuela's wake was in the living room of her house. They brought us over, and my aunt lifted me up and made me kiss her. She was very cold! After that, I got so scared that every time I went over there, I could not be by myself in their living room. The vision of her in the casket and the memory of the coldness I felt when I kissed her always came into my mind. I do not recommend anyone doing this to a child!

Everything was going great for my mother until my grandmother passed away. When we got to the house after the funeral, Edelmira had all of the windows and doors open and was playing loud music while cleaning the house. My father was very upset about the lack of respect she was showing and how she was making us look in front of all of the neighbors. He almost fired her at that moment.

Then Edelmira was using our comb. My mother had told her many times that she did not want her to use our comb, and she even gave her one, but she continued using ours. One day, my mother noticed that Edelmira was scratching her head. My mom looked closer and saw she had lice. When my mother checked our heads, all of us had lice! My mother began crying because she did not know how to treat it. She contacted my grandmother Aurora, who came to give her a helping hand. They cleaned our hair with kerosene for several days to kill the lice. After all of this commotion, Edelmira was finally let go. We helped our mother clean the house.

After work, my father began going out with friends to a bar across the street from the store. He would have a few beers and appetizers there. By the time he got home around 9:00 p.m., and sometimes past that time, we were already in bed. My mom had the dining room table all set for him to have dinner. At that point, he did not feel like eating, and this upset my mother. She had to throw the food away, which she had been warming all that time. All of this ended after the store was expropriated and he did not have enough money to go out with his friends. My mother was happy about it. Pipo was also a heavy smoker, and I remember him rocking us and smoking. My mom never smoked, but definitely got secondhand smoke.

Chapter
10

In those years, my mom also had a cook named Felicia, who did not take good care of herself. Her heels looked dirty, and she did not smell clean, but my mother kept her because she really knew how to cook Spanish meals.

After Mirtica was born, my mother started noticing that the food was not lasting very long, and she had to go grocery shopping more frequently than before. We, the girls, noticed that when Felicia was getting to work, she came without any breasts and left with big ones. We mentioned this to Mima, and she began watching her too. We also noticed that when she brought the metal garbage can out, she made noises on the side of the can.

Later on, we saw her alcoholic son come and take a bag from inside the garbage can. My mother confronted her and asked her why her son was coming to the garbage can. She said she did not know. My mom told Felicia that if she needed some food, she could help her with that, but she told her not to take it. She also felt bad about firing her because she knew she was the one supporting her son and grandson. After that, she came one day and told my mother that she had found another job with better pay and left. We were so glad she was gone.

Above, Mima is sitting holding Julita, and Marita and I are sitting on the floor. I was always making jokes and acting like I did not do anything, but Marita always got in trouble for laughing silly at them. That's what happened in this picture. Julita has a cut above her eye because she stood in front of the swing after I pushed Marita, and she knocked her down, causing Julita to hit her face against the metal garbage can that was in the corner. We had to take her to the emergency room for stitches. Poor girl! In the next picture, my father is with Julita. Mima is pregnant with Mirtica. Standing are Marita, me, and Margarita. We were coming back from school, which is the reason why we still had our uniforms on.

 Old houses in Cuba do not have closets, so families need to have wardrobes to keep their clothes. My parents had this one in their bedroom. I am sharing this picture of me in my parents' bedroom, combing

my hair, so you can see the wardrobe they had in their bedroom. I believe I was ten years old then.

Floors were all tiled, and rooms had glass double doors called "portieles" to separate the rooms from each other and provide more privacy.

This house was haunted! Four of us were sleeping in the second bedroom, which had double doors and double windows to the patio. The windows were really doors, but they had iron bars on them, so you could only open them and let the breeze come in. Because of the bars, nobody was able to get in the house, except insects. Remember, all of these houses were about a hundred years old, and there was no air conditioning. That was the reason why most of these houses had bars on their windows that were as tall as doors. They were row houses that had windows and doors that opened to the interior courtyard. We could keep all of them open during the hot days.

In that bedroom, we had Julita's toddler bed against the wall, and there was a double bed in the middle and a twin bed against the other wall. Nightstands separated the beds. A vanity with a long mirror, two drawers, and a bench was placed between the double doors and the double floor window. Julita was in a small child's bed, Marita and Margarita were sleeping in the double bed, and I was sleeping by myself in the twin bed. Mirtica slept in her crib in my parents' bedroom.

One night, the moon was very bright, and I began hearing steps approach my bed. The shining moon kept the room lighted through the open doors of the window. All of a sudden, I felt like someone was against the footboard of my bed. I opened my eyes and saw the figure of a man wearing a brown suit and a hat. I covered my head again, and I heard him walking toward the headboard, leaning toward me. I kept my head covered, but I could feel

61

his proximity. I began screaming, and that spirit ran away. I woke up everyone in the house. My heart was beating very fast when I told my mother what had happened. She stayed in bed with me until I fell sleep again. At the end of the week, the owner of the house came to collect the rent, and my mother was showing her the way she placed the furniture in the house. I was next to her when she told my mother that my bed was in the same place where she had her father's bed when he died. My mom asked her if he was buried wearing a brown suit and a hat, and she said yes.

As I mentioned before, we still could hear my grandmother Zoila's steps through the house. I asked my sister Marita if she could hear what was happening, and she said yes, and Margarita could too. Both of my parents could hear her steps, so it was not my imagination. We got so scared in that house that we were afraid to be alone in any of the rooms, and when the night came, the noises got worse and we could not sleep. My father decided to find another place to live because we all thought that the house was haunted.

Remember, when Aunt Marta divorced Mario, she moved back into my grandparents' house, and her ex-husband's sister Ramona moved into that house with her daughter Violetica. Since this house shared the central courtyard, Violetica was always playing with us. I remember one day at the beach house when we were playing on a pile of sand that was being used for the houses they were building across the street. While my mother was watching us, she noticed that Margarita was missing. Well, Violetica had buried her in the sand! Thank God my mom was able to get her out in time. We were all scared, and Violetica's mother reprimanded her. Unfortunately, Violetica died about three years ago in Miami.

Here are the first cousins who grew up together at the beach house and celebrated Mayito's birthday: Mirtica, Nery, Alberto, Julita, Chito, Mayito, Tatoño, Violetica, Margarita, and Marita

62

Years later, we moved to the same block where the Archdiocese of Matanzas was. The Instituto de Matanzas, a school we later attended for a year, was on the next block. It was next to the corner of Contreras and Compostela. It was a very small place: a living room, a dining area, two bedrooms, a very small bathroom, and a kitchen with no side wall, which was open to a little square patio. It was not too far from where the one on America Street was. Can you imagine the seven of us in such small place? Mirtica had her crib in my parents' bedroom, and the four of us slept in the next room (two girls to a twin bed). Perhaps this is the reason why I always feel better in bigger houses, and thank God my husband and I have been able to have beautiful, spacious places for our family to enjoy during all of the years we have been married. At this place, one day my baby sister Mirta woke up crying and had blood on one of her hands; a rat had bit her! My parents took her to the doctor, and he ordered rabies shots. Poor Mirtica endured those ten shots in her back when she was only a year and a half old.

Our aunts Irma and Mirta kept taking us on weekends to spend some time with them and our grandparents. Sometimes we went out with their cousins from out of town. We visited many nice places. When they went to Havana to visit our relatives there, they took us too. We also went to their uncle, aunt, and family in Navajas, a suburb in the city Pedro Betancourt, which was about two hours from Matanzas. I will tell you about this place later on in my story.

When Tia Mirta was taking sewing classes, she took me with her one day. I loved what they were doing and showed a lot of interest. I went again with her the next Saturday, and the teacher had me do some patterns and some miniature dresses. I did it so well for my age—only thirteen—that she told my aunt that she did not have to pay for my lessons, as she was giving me a scholarship.

I learned how to sew!!

Chapter
11

In Cuba, before Castro's educational changes, high school went up to eighth grade, and from there you attended a vocational/technical school according to what you wanted to do in life. At the age of eighteen, you were ready to teach or work in an office with an accounting degree, or you could have a trade or a bachelor's degree in science to study medicine or any other career at the university level. I feel that education then was deeper and more complete, and high school children were treated with respect and acted more mature.

Marita and I tried the entrance exam for the Normal School for Teachers. I scored second place in the private school group. I missed first place by a tenth of a point, and my friend Ester Alicia got it. Since I was underaged, my parents had to get special permission from the school in order for me to attend this school. Marita always got very nervous when taking any test, and sadly she did not pass this exam.

Then Marita wanted to try the entrance exam for the Professional School of Commerce. She asked me if I could go with her at night, as she was working at the store during the day. She wanted me to go with her to this school. We both passed this exam; therefore, I went during the day to the school for teachers, and at night I went to the commerce school. She worked at the store with my father during the day. We both graduated from this school and received degrees in accounting. I also graduated from the other school as a primary school teacher.

In the United States, Marita always worked in accounting, using the skills she learned at the Professional School of Commerce in Cuba. Even after she retired, she was asked by the owners of the company to come back and train the new personnel, because she was the most knowledgeable worker in that department. She had worked for so many years in the same distributing company that she knew better than anybody else how to manage the department. But she got tired of all of the driving and Miami traffic, so she decided to stay at home and enjoy her full-time retirement.

During the years at the Normal School for Teachers and the accounting school, I was part of their bands as a drum majorette. I enjoyed the practices, the marching, and doing twirl movements. I was in my early teenager years!

The shock was when the new so-called socialist system, which immediately became a communist government, changed the entire educational system. These schools were eventually closed, and all of the fun was gone. They closed the Normal School for Teachers first, and at the accounting school, many of the teachers began coming to teach in their olive-green soldier uniforms. It became a very intimidating situation.

I remember when one of them, the political science professor—this was the last subject I had to pass to receive my diploma—told me that I passed his subject with a C because I wrote very well, but he totally disagreed with my point of view on the subject. He had given three questions to answer, all of them based on the Marxist/Leninist theories and my thoughts about the Castro Revolution. I wrote what my heart dictated, and I am happy that at least I was able to pass this awful course and finish my career. I was able to graduate from both schools.

Two years after Fidel Castro took power, in 1961, he decided to close the Normal School for Teachers. Teachers had to go to a boarding school in Havana, where they received special communist doctrine training, as they were the ones who had to indoctrinate the children in school. They were called the pioneers. The students who were close to finishing their degrees had to spend a year alphabetizing adults in the countryside.

I was able to do only some of the alphabetization program in Cuban's fields. The books Castro's revolution made us use were designed to indoctrinate these adults, teaching them about socialism/communism, teaching them how great Fidel Castro was, along with other members of the revolution, and using the letters of the alphabet to teach them the names of military equipment. Because I began developing hypothyroidism and was feeling tired and depressed, I had to quit the alphabetization program, with a doctor's permission, of course.

Many of us were not able to go through this program and could not receive our degrees. In 1965, my father's first cousin Roberto, who was the director of this program and was incorporated in the revolution, decided to give another opportunity to all of us, and he created an addendum that said we had to pass a special teaching battery of tests in order to receive our teaching degrees. Several of my friends and I studied very hard. We wanted to graduate and become teachers. Estelita, Maria Elena, Esperancita, and I did not rest, even on weekends, as were studying to pass these tests. About ten of us successfully passed them and received our teaching degrees in 1966.

As you can see, the diploma has a different name. It says Escuela de Superación Pedagógica Nguyen Van Troi (a Vietnamese Communist martyr) instead of Escuela Normal de Maestros.

I was also able to finish the accounting school Escuela Professional de Comercio, and I received a degree from there too. In the United States, I was able to work as a teacher's assistant in Worcester, Massachusetts, when I first arrived, and then I worked as assistant to the comptroller at Maru Distributing Company when we moved to Miami. I revalidated my teaching degree and taught at an adult basic education program from 1975 to my retirement. My specialty was mathematics.

During all of that time, I was also taking piano lessons and finished music theory. Then, later on, I began attending L'Alliance Francaise in Havana but was not able to complete the fifth year, but I was already fluent in French. I always needed to have a book in my hands!

The legacy that our parents left us was an excellent education, and the communists could not take that away from us.

Chapter 12

Many youngsters lived in the new area where we moved. Ayuntamiento Street was almost at the corner with Compostela, and we made a lot of new friends. Fulgencio Batista was the president of the republic then, and we witnessed a shooting at the Institute of Matanzas's sidewalk, which was only one block away. My father called us to the door when this was happening, and we witnessed what the soldiers were doing. I saw a young man sitting on the sidewalk, begging for his life, and the soldier got his gun and shot at him several times to make sure he was dead. It was a horrible experience. He did not have a chance for justice. That took place in December of 1958.

Marita reminded me that our father did not want us to dance. Pipo used to tell us that dancing was a public embrace, and he did not want to see his daughters in that situation. When we went to the dances that took place at the girls' homes, our mother took us, and our father was watching us by the window, making sure we were not dancing cheek to cheek or too close to the guys. He even taught us how to put our left arm on the guys' chests to keep them away when dancing. One time when I was dancing, out of nowhere my father came in and told the guy to keep his distance. I could not believe it! That was a very embarrassing moment.

Our mother was our hero. She always had a positive attitude through all adversities. I still remember the day I took my mom to the doctor and he told her that she had pulmonary fibrosis and only had between three to five years of life. He said that the ending would be horrible. She was only seventy-seven years old. My mom told him then that he was not God and couldn't know how many years of life she had left, that God was the only one who knew. I was in shock because I did not expect this doctor to tell her something like that in such a rude manner, and in a very heartbreaking way. I felt badly for her, but she kept her positive attitude, thank God.

Here she is at the beginning of her sickness.

Before that, while we were waiting for the doctor to come to see her, we heard him telling an older lady who was there by herself that she was on her last leg and was going to die soon. Mima and I could not believe the inhuman way this doctor was telling this old lady that she was in her last days. At least I was there with my mother when he broke the news. That was the last day we went to that doctor, because she did not want to see him again.

At the end of her sickness, she began having lack of oxygen in her brain, which gave her some form of dementia. The last year of her life, she had to have her bottom teeth removed because she had problems swallowing her medications, and the cortisone she had to chew affected the gums. I still feel that the dentists she saw

70

should have treated her gums instead of having her teeth removed, especially at her age and condition. That affected her eating and changed the shape of her mouth. They wanted to remove all of her teeth, but I stopped the procedure and took her home. Mima was very thankful that I made that decision. I was the one taking her to the doctors most of the time, as all of my sisters were working, and I was the only one available. She died at the age of eighty-four, seven years after her diagnosis.

I have to tell you that my mother was very sweet and romantic. She was a poet, a singer, and a music composer. I inherited these talents from her, and our son Marc did too. All of my sisters sing, but especially Mirtica, who has a beautiful soprano voice. She is very artistic, and she plays the piano, paints, and writes poetry. She is the most artistic one of us all!

I just have to add that I enjoyed working with my mother to record our musical compositions before she was sick. I paid for all of our recordings and do not regret it one bit. We began participating in musical festivals and won several of them. This was something that we shared with each other. My father was not too happy with this, but thank God I had the support of my husband. He stayed home taking care of the children. I would go with Mima after work to the recording studio to get our songs recorded by Nestor. I sang our songs, and many times I was so exhausted. She did some of the choruses and told me what she wanted us to add or change. We had great times together.

Going back to the problems in Cuba, the political situation began to get worse, and we were even afraid to go to parties or just go out. Groups were already formed to get rid of Batista. They were collecting weapons for the revolution. Our next-door neighbor was hiding a mattress full of them in his house.

My father was afraid of what was happening, worried we would go out and get hurt. He then decided to look for a bigger house in the center of the city of Matanzas, near the downtown area, which was where the store was, so it was easier for him to go to work. It was also closer to our private school, La Virgen Milagrosa. He could walk my sisters to school! The address was Rio #42 Altos. This was an old colonial Spanish house, about one hundred years old. We lived in the upstairs, which had a formal living room, a family room, three bedrooms, a dining room next to the kitchen, and one and a half bathrooms. It also had a third floor with two bedrooms and a patio that had stairs to the terrace. This house had a long street balcony from the living room to the main bedroom, and it faced the upstairs of the Arturo Echemendia private school. There were double doors for hurricane prevention. One was made of solid wood, and the other one was made with vertical blinds.

This house had beautiful colonial paintings around the bottom part of the walls in the living room, which matched the paintings on the glass of the "portiel" (ornamental interior doors with decorative glass that give some privacy to another room) in my parents' bedroom. My father gave instructions to paint the living room walls above these beautiful paintings. To his surprise, when he went to check on the work these men were doing, they had painted over all of the living room walls. All of those beautiful paintings were gone!

Finally, the news came on January 1, 1959, that Dictator Fulgencio Batista had left and Fidel Castro's group was coming to take over. The TV news reporters were announcing what was going on, keeping the people informed. At home, my parents were happy this was happening. Finally, Cuba was going to have a democratic leader and elections! Who was going to tell us that the people were so wrong and naïve? Fidel Castro played along with what the people

72

wanted. He did not show his real colors until almost two years later. Everything changed then!

We moved into that house in the middle of 1959. My mother found a Spanish cook who lived in the area. Her name was Gilda. She was in her fifties, maybe sixties, and was single. She had gray hair, but she surely knew how to cook. To our surprise and amusement, every month she came with a different hair color. She made a hair dye, sometimes with mercurochrome, for red. She used iodine for blond and gentian violet for purple! You never knew what it was going to be. She was like a chameleon! One day when she came, we were watching a soap opera on TV, and she began watching it. Suddenly, she screamed, "Oh, my God, I saw him kissing another woman the other day!" It was an actor who worked in different shows, and she believed it was real.

My father bought a lot of new furniture for this nice place, including an upright piano. I began taking piano lessons at Condon Ruiz de la Torre Music Academy. We were all thrilled and enjoyed it. It was just two blocks from the central park, where we had great times with old and new friends.

After we were established in that house, I remember that one day my father invited his first cousin Joaquinito, who was a lawyer in town, and his wife, Irene, who was a pharmacist, over for dinner. Joaquinito and Irene did not have any children, but they were my sister Julita's godparents. My mother prepared a very elegant table for them and all of us. Gilda, our cook, made a delicious Spanish dinner of "arroz con mariscos" (rice with all types of fish), salad, and "tostones" (green plantain cut in one-inch rolls, smashed and fried). There was wine for the adults and sodas for us, and for dessert my mother made a flan.

When we were all seated around the table of our new dining room set, my mother noticed that we needed more arroz con mariscos at the table. My mom asked Gilda to bring more rice while giving her the empty tray. Instead of serving the rice from the tray, she came into the dining room with the large pot under her arm and began walking around the table, asking who wanted more rice. My mom began signaling for her not to do that. All of the girls began laughing and could not stop. We were spilling what we had in our mouths all over the table. At that point, my father sent us all to our bedrooms. That was the end of that dinner for us. Today, we still laugh at the memory of that moment.

Later on, when the government left my father without a job, he could not pay Gilda anymore. Gilda still wanted to continue coming and helping. That way, she could have something better to eat and could still enjoy our company. Unfortunately, the lady she was living with moved away, and she had to leave too. It was very sad to see her go. She did not have anybody else in Matanzas, but she had a brother in Oriente, Cuba. She had become part of our family, and we hated to see her go. She moved away to be with her brother.

Chapter 13

On January 8, 1959, people were on the streets to see the trucks passing by, full of bearded men coming down from the mountains to take over the government. Everybody was cheering, shouting, and waving flags, handkerchiefs, and whatever they could display. People were happy and were dreaming about a new democratic government. I was still young, but I could see, feel, and sense their happiness, and I was also there cheering with them.

Ed Sullivan interviewed Fidel Castro on January 11, 1959, in our city of Matanzas, Cuba, shortly after the Batista regime was overthrown during the Cuban Revolution. Castro affirmed him that he was bringing a democratic government to Cuba, that he was not a communist. In Ed Sullivan's interview, he mentioned that Fidel Castro was the people's idol—someone who was going to bring the Cubans freedom and justice—and that there was a new light in the horizon. A democratic government! Finally, we were rid of a dictator! At least we thought so. Manuel Urrutia was appointed as the president of the Republic of Cuba, while Fidel became the prime minister.

In 1959, the first law that was enacted was the **Agrarian Reform**, which limited the amount of land someone could own, and any land owned above that limit was expropriated by the government, including the animals. Militia groups were formed, and soldiers were marching on our streets, shouting slogans. A year later, when things took a turn for the worst, my friends and I used to make fun of the slogans, saying: "Uno, dos, tres, cuatro, comiendo mierda, rompiendo zapatos, si suena un tiro, no queda ni un gato." (One, two, three, four, eating shit, breaking your shoes, if a shot is fired, not even a cat remains.) Believe me, it sounds better in Spanish!

In July of the same year, President Urrutia resigned, and Osvaldo Dorticos was appointed as the president of the Republic of Cuba. These two were presidents in name only, as they did not have any say in what was taking place. Everything was orchestrated by Fidel. Nobody knew what Fidel's real intentions were, or what kind of government he wanted to bring to the island. Fidel Castro was president from 1976 to 2008. He also served as the commander in chief of the Cuban Revolutionary Armed Forces.

During 1959, thousands of executions were ordered by Che Guevara, a communist Argentinian who fought with Fidel in the mountains of Escambray. He was in charge of the firing squads' killings. The majority of the executions were conducted without due process and a fair trial. Nowadays, you can see Che t-shirts being worn by imbeciles who don't even know who he was. They see him as a folk hero, and that boils my blood. What happened to the democracy we were offered?

Equally important, the government began the slogan "Armas, ¿para qué?" This meant, "Firearms, what for?" Therefore, some citizens began to turn in their arms voluntarily. Shortly after, the government passed a law against the **Right to Bear Arms**. People had to turn in their guns, and all of the weapons were confiscated. The government's idea was to disarm the people so they could not have a way to defend themselves when other abominable laws were imposed. The firing squads continued killing people without trials,

76

and if all of the government's actions were not to the liking of the people, they could not defend themselves or protest.

Children attending public schools were also told to march when going to lunch or when moving from one place to another. This was not happening in the private schools that were still in existence. Nobody knew what was coming. Cubans were so naive to believe it was a democracy.

In January of 1960, radio and TV stations were seized, along with all of the newspapers and magazines, limiting the **Freedom of Speech** and expression. Today, there are several channels on the island with the same communistic theme, one of them a musical one and another one with programs from a series. There is also a foreign one from a different country. All of these channels show programs that are only approved by the government. Actually, those people who can afford it have illegal TV antennae and cards, which can be purchased at the high cost of about $40 dollars a month. This is something only the elite, or those who have families in the US, can afford. You can see many channels. The few who have the unaffordable internet can even watch Netflix on tablets given to them by family or friends in the USA, but all of that is expensive for the regular citizen. The average salary is about $9 a month. *Granma* is the national newspaper and brings the people only the news approved by the government, and small local newspapers are the same. In Cuba today, 90 percent of its citizens live in poverty.

In July of the same year, all US businesses and commercial properties were nationalized, and by October, all of the Cuban-owned private businesses and rental properties were also seized, along with commercial bank accounts. **The abolition of private property and free enterprise began**. It was a forced expropriation without compensation! Here it comes, the redistribution of wealth!

The United States imposed an embargo prohibiting all exports to Cuba except food and medical supplies.

One day in December of 1960, at 5:00 a.m., we were awakened by a loud knocking at the front door of our house. The door was downstairs, but it could be opened from upstairs, where our living area was. My father thought that someone had died in the family! When the door was opened, we heard heavy, booted footsteps coming up the stairs. They were soldiers! We were frightened! Were they coming to take my father away? When they got upstairs, my father approached them, and they asked, "Are you Antonio Barnet?" After his affirmative reply, he was asked to turn over the keys to the business that he managed. It was an apparel fabric store called La Casa Verde (The Green House). They proceeded to tell him to be at work at 8:00 a.m.

My father did what he was told, and when he got to the store, to my father's surprise, our old cleaning lady, Edelmira—the one that gave us lice—was the manager. She said to him, "How do you like it, Barnet? I am now your boss, and you need to teach me what I need to know." He told her that he was going to do his best but that he was not sure if she could learn everything he learned over years of working in that place. My father continued working there under those circumstances, receiving a very low government salary, but he had to do it in order to support our family. After he presented documentation to the government asking permission to leave the country, he was laid off in 1965. In fact, the government laid off all of the people who asked permission to leave the country. Since all of the businesses had been confiscated by the government, the government was the one employing or firing you, so if you presented your desire to leave the country, you were out of a job.

During 1960, the **Committees of Defense of the Revolution (CDR) were established**, neighbors spying on neighbors.

78

Some of our neighbors were part of this block committee, and they were taking turns day and night, watching what was going on on the block. If they saw something that was suspicious to them, or if they thought there was something against the revolution, you were then reported to the police. This was happening on every block! When Fidel Castro gave his speeches, which lasted for hours, the presidents of the block committees put speakers on every block to force the people to listen to his speech. There were moments when we felt like screaming at them to shut it off. Fidel's new slogan was "Patria o Muerte, Venceremos," which meant "Country or Death, We Will Conquer." Signs with this slogan can be found all over the island.

Around this time, many parents were sending their children to the USA alone, using a Catholic program called **Operation Peter Pan**, to avoid the school socialist/communist indoctrination that was beginning to take place. Fourteen thousand children of parents opposed to the system were sent to the USA to avoid indoctrination. My parents were able to obtain USA visas through this program to send their three oldest daughters first—Marita, Margarita, and me—with the idea that they would follow after with the smaller ones. Immigration from Cuba to the USA was halted by Castro in 1962.

About ten thousand Peter Pan children were trapped in Cuba, unable to leave, and we were among them. Many parents who were hoping to be reunited with their children soon were kept behind, and it took many of them years to be able to leave, and others could never do so. In a way, my father was glad we had stayed behind, because he was afraid to send us into the unknown so young, alone. He regretted it, though, years later, when Margarita left alone and I was sent to the forced labor camps.

Our friend and neighbor Alina, age fourteen, and her younger brother Aldo, age seven, are pictured below. They were leaving through the Peter Pan program. I remember how hard it was for their parents to let them go. A group of their friends went to the airport to say goodbye to them. A few years later, their parents left. It took us thirty-five years to see Alina again, but we never saw her brother Aldo, as he passed away at a young age in Miami.

On the right: Margarita, Nery, and Alina celebrating Nery's birthday in 2019 at Bolero in Miami.

Chapter

14

Before Castro, about 80 percent of Cuba's population was literate. This was the fourth highest rate in Latin America according to the UNESCO. The educational system was different. We had free public education through elementary, secondary, and adult level, plus private and religious schools, which you had to pay for unless you had a scholarship. You went to school up to the eighth-grade level, and you already studied trigonometry in math. It was a very advanced educational system, like finishing high school at eighth grade. From there, you could go to different specialized fields like accounting, teaching, and arts, and there were also polytechnical schools, or "bachilleratos" (post-secondary), for those who wanted to become engineers, doctors, lawyers, etc.

Those students who went to the Professional School of Commerce or the Normal School for Teachers started working in their careers, accounting or teaching, at the early age of eighteen or nineteen. The ones who wanted to continue and have a more advanced career had to go to the university. Others just found a job in the career they had chosen, like teaching, accounting, bookkeeping, etc. I believe that youngsters then displayed more maturity and were more disciplined. They were ready for work.

As I mentioned before, I was a year ahead in school, so when I finished eighth grade, I was only twelve years old. My parents had to get special permission from the educational department in order for me to take the general ability exam preparation course. I was not old enough to go into the needed course and prepare for the entry exam for the Normal School for Teachers. I scored second place by a tenth of a point. My friend Ester Alicia got first place in the private school group. The following year, when I began the teaching and commerce schools, I was only thirteen years old. I was the youngest one in my class! I was attending the teaching school during the day and the accounting school at night so I could go with my sister Marita. She was working with my father at the clothing store during the day and attending school at night. Anyway, I always liked math.

In this picture, you can see me with a dog called Fifina. I went to a school party and saw this poor puppy crying. I took it home that day, and she lived with us for thirteen years, until we had to leave the country. She was one more girl in the  family. She even slept with us! When it was our time to leave the country, we left her with our next door neighbor. It was so sad to have to leave her behind. Unfortunately, the lady who took her in died a year later, and her husband took our dear, spoiled Fifina to a farm working camp and left her there, forcing her to sleep outdoors. He told another neighbor that at least she could get something to eat from the people doing farming there. Just thinking that the last years of her life were miserable still breaks my heart.

A memorable, comical incident that is etched into my mind happened at the graduation ceremony of the Normal School for

Teachers in 1960. It was happening at Sauto Theater, where my friend Estelita was playing the piano while Daisy and I were doing a duet, singing "La Bayamesa," a Cuban song. As soon as we began singing, I saw this heavy guy approaching one of the balcony seats. He was getting ready to sit down. I was singing but watching him, as I was staring at one place so I would not get nervous while singing in front of so many people. When he sat down, the chair broke, and he went all the way to the floor. It sounded like a bomb went off!

People began screaming, scared because of the sound. They did not know what had happened. But since I saw what happened, I began laughing, out of control and unable to stop. The director of the show closed the curtains, but after a little while, he opened them again so we could continue. But I began laughing again and could not control myself. The curtains were closed for good then. That was the end of our show. Today, Estelita and I still laugh about it when we talk to each other. Daisy stayed away from me because she got very involved in the revolution. I guess she was also upset at me because I could not stop laughing the day of our show. She really wanted to shine while singing!

Years later, Daisy became my sister Mirtica's third grade teacher at the public school. She was integrated into the revolution and disliked my sister because she knew we were not of the same ideals. She mistreated her, ridiculed her in front of the class, and pulled her up by the ears from her seat so often that it caused her headaches and earaches. She was abusive! My mom and I went to the school to speak to the principal about this situation, and she told my mom she was going to see what she could do. On my way out, I stopped in her classroom and told Daisy in front of her class that if she continued doing this to my sister, she was going to know who I really was. I told her she better stop mistreating her. Mirtica said that because of what I said to her teacher in front of the class,

83

I became her hero. Daisy stopped bothering her, and we stayed away from each other.

The Normal School for Teachers was closed by the government in 1961, and if you wanted to continue your career, you had to go to Makarenko School for Teachers,  a school in Havana that was created by Castro in order to prepare teachers for the new school curriculum that was dictated by the Revolution. It was going to be introduced in all schools. This curriculum imposed the socialist Marxist ideals the government was imposing.

At this school, Castro was trying a new educational system in which productive labor was incorporated, following the Soviet Union system created by Anton Makarenko. These teachers were going to be trained to enforce this system. For many years, students in Cuba had to do agricultural work during their scholastic education, up until they graduated from the university. These agricultural programs were put into action in 1967 and ended in 2012. I will be more descriptive about this program later in the book.

We were young, never thinking about what was coming. For the students who were in their last year at the Normal School for Teachers, a program was created to help us achieve our degrees. We had to go to the hills and farms to alphabetize the farmers. I received the literacy books and could not believe what I was seeing. All of the letters referred to the revolution. It was pure indoctrination. Example: A–Armas (arms, weapons), B–Botas (boots),

C–Castro, Ch–Che (referring to the killer Che Guevara), D–Desfile, F–Fusil, Y–Yanqui, etc.

I had to stop alphabetizing during the third week due to a health issue I had that was not being treated. It was much better for me not to be teaching something I believed was indoctrination. Later on, in 1965, one of my father's cousins, who was director of the educational department in Matanzas, gave an opportunity to students like me, who could not participate in the program and could not go to rural areas to alphabetize, that allowed us to take an intense program that had final testings in pedagogy, literacy, and demagogy, among other subjects. A team of friends got together, and we studied very hard to graduate! Among them were Estelita, Maria Elena, and Esperanza. Finally, we were able to take those tests and receive our teaching degrees. I received an accounting degree the following year. These degrees were very beneficial for me during my life. I went back to school in the USA and received my bachelor's and master's degrees. I went back to the university again to obtain my specialist degree in education. I am a retired teacher now.

I could not have the sweet fifteen party I was dreaming of having. I just had a cake and wore a pink dress Aunt Ina made for me. Some of my close friends came over, and we danced and had a good time. We could not have a big celebration because our great-grandmother Maria Néstora (we called her Abuelita) had passed away the month before. In those days, my father's family was very strict about keeping to the customs of mourning for several years, dressing in black and not going anywhere. Also, the country's situation at that moment was getting worse. My parents made sure I had a nice studio picture taken, but something I hate from this picture is the hat (pamela) the photographer insisted that I should hold.

Marita, who did not have her sweet fifteen big party, did not have a studio picture taken then, either. Our mother took us to a studio, and we both had these beautiful pictures done the same day. She was sixteen and a half years old and beautiful.

Chapter 15

In the beginning of the sixties, we were teenagers and enjoyed going to the beach, parties, and our dear park. On weekends, our city park—called Parque de la Libertad because it has a statue of a lady who symbolizes freedom and a statue of Apostle Jose Marti—was the meeting place for all youngsters. Castro's government put a fence around it, as you can see in the picture, to prevent people from getting close to the statue. It used to be surrounded by steps going up to the statue.

We sat, talked, laughed, walked around, and sat on a bench. The curious thing about it was that on Saturdays, girls always walked around, making a circle around the perimeter of the park, and at the same time the boys were walking on the outside circle, going the opposite way. We loved to do that so we could see the boys we liked when they passed us around the circle. If we liked them, they then joined us in the girls' circle and talked to us, or we would all get out of the circle to sit on one of the benches.

On Sundays, they had the symphonic band playing nice music while we were walking around the circle. No dancing was involved, but we walked, talked, laughed, and had pure fun. This was a custom that took place for many years, until Castro, but it continued almost until we left.

The sad thing was that many of our friends kept leaving the country, with or without their families. Some were able to take some of their jewelry by sewing pieces into their dresses' hems, or wearing them in their hair, so they were not detected. This happened at the beginning, but later on, we were not allowed to bring anything because security got worse. Many left alone through the Peter Pan program, like Alina, who left with her brother Aldo, because their family did not have visas to leave yet.

Some of those children never saw their parents again because they were jailed, died, or were never allowed to leave Cuba. In this picture are Margarita, Alina, Armonía, and I. Soon after, Armonía left with Jorge, her younger brother, for Barcelona in Spain. Her mother joined them years later.

When the majority of my friends had left the country and I was feeling so lonely, I began going out to the beach, the park, and parties with my younger sisters' friends. The funny thing was that they called me the youngster (la juvenil)! My mom was glad that I was keeping an eye on my sisters, even though we always went out with a chaperone. Sometimes it was another friend's mom or aunt, or our own mother, but we always went with a chaperone. That was the way then. When I came to the US and began going out with Bob, it was the first time I went out without a chaperone. By then, I was old enough to know how to take care of myself. We got married in less than a year.

The Pioneer Program was imposed at all elementary schools after **all of the private and religious schools were seized.** This is the reason why so many parents sent their children away, alone, through the Peter Pan program. Teachers were trained under the Youth Communist Doctrine.

Two of my sisters, Julita and Mirtica, were attending the elementary school. They suffered the pain of the closing of the private school they were attending, La Virgen Milagrosa, and they were placed into the public school, which had a communist educational system. The school was located on the same block as our home. It was called Anexa School, but its name was changed after the educational reform, and that building is gone today. **The Forces of Pioneer in Action Program**, where children were assigned to social and working tasks around school, began.

My sister Mirtica was very affected by the closing of the Catholic school and could not stand going to this new public one. She was in the first grade. One day, our parents were called to school to discuss Mirtica's behavior. She told the principal that she hated the school and that she had a bomb in her pocket. The principal called my parents and wanted to know why she was using that kind of language, wondering if that type of conversation was taking place at home. My parents got very scared after hearing that. They thought they were going to be reprimanded with jail for this. Thank God that the principal knew my father, and he told him to tell my sister not to repeat that again. She was influenced badly, because in those years, different bombs detonated in the area because of the counterrevolutionaries.

When I was going to the Normal School for Teachers, we did our practices at the Anexa School, presenting our lessons to the students in front of a group of other future teachers and the classroom teacher. They observed you and wrote their critiques, which would be discussed on a later day. All of that changed after they closed the school and all of the private schools.

After the Normal School for Teachers was closed, my friend Estelita and I began attending the Alliance Francaise Ecole (French Alliance School) in Havana on Saturdays. We heard about this school from our friend Ester Alicia. She was already taking these classes. Estelita insisted that we go, saying that it was going to be fun to learn another language. In the beginning, she was driving us there in her car (she the only one of my girlfriends who had a car), but later on, when the gasoline was limited, we began going by bus. One day, we decided to do something different. We took the Hershey train to Regla, a city across from the Havana Bay, and we took a boat that took us across the bay. We walked to school from there. After that trip, we decided not to go that way again, as we had to walk through some neighborhoods that were not too great, and it also involved a long walking distance.

We always went to the Hilton Hotel, which was later changed to Havana Libre, to have lunch after class, and sometimes we went to the movie theater. Estelita was and still is a very well-mannered lady. After lunch, we always ordered éclairs for dessert. She took her fork and knife and began cutting hers. I usually grabbed mine and ate it, but after I saw her doing that, I began doing the same thing. Well, what a surprise it was when my éclair went flying off my plate and ended up in the middle of the hall! We began laughing uncontrollably.

On another day when we were having lunch at the Hilton, I ordered enchilado de camarones (shrimp creole) over rice. When I began cutting the shrimp, it was so hard that a bunch of rice and shrimp, plus the sauce, landed on my skirt. I looked at Estelita's face, and she was red from embarrassment, and she said, "What are you going to do now?" I smiled back at her and stood up, and all of the shrimp and rice fell on the floor. She could not believe what I had done! But what else could I have done? I walked to the bathroom to clean my skirt, which was kind of impossible to do. That sauce left a tremendous stain! I went back to the table, and we paid our bills and left. We were quiet on the bus going back home. We surely enjoyed these trips to Havana. It was something different to do on Saturdays. One time, we visited one of her aunts, who lived in a beautiful condominium facing Havana Harbor. Estelita was able to leave Cuba in 1966. She was lucky not to have to go through the forced labor camps like I did. We still laugh while reminiscing about some of those things that happened when we were young.

I visited Los Angeles in October of 2019. We got together with my friends Estelita and Armonía, and her brother Jorge, who is a neurologist in Los Angeles. He left Cuba when he was only ten years old. We had a wonderful time visiting  different places and having dinners at different restaurants. It was great to see them again after so many years.

Here I am with Armonía and Estelita.

Chapter

16

The year of 1961 was very stressful for all of us. Remember that my sister Marita and I graduated from La Virgen Milagrosa Catholic School and were, at that point, attending the commerce school at night, and I was also attending the teaching school during the day. My sister Margarita graduated that year from the Catholic school, but my other two sisters, Julita and Mirtica, were still attending there when it was confiscated. This school was also a convent of the charity nuns. All of the private schools were confiscated, and when this happened, all of the nuns were sent into exile, including the ones at our school. Our school was ransacked, and the beautiful chapel where we took communion, sang, and went to mass was destroyed. So much hate against religions! This was the saddest thing for the students to see! One of the nuns came to our home because she was able to save the Lord's oil painting, which had been at the school entry, and was bringing it for my mother to keep. When the time for us to leave was getting closer, my father took the painting, in a disguised way, to another family because one of its members was going to stay in Cuba, and she was a devoted Catholic. You can see the beautiful chapel in this picture I am sharing with you. I am the angel on the right.

On April 17, 1961, the **Bay of Pigs Invasion** took place in Playa Giron. Prior to the invasion, during the term of President Eisenhower, he had authorized the CIA to start an invasion force of Cuban exiles in Miami, which would hopefully bring down the government of Fidel Castro. The exiles were trained in Guatemala. The invasion plans were turned over to the Kennedy administration. Before the operation could be executed, Castro learned from his informers about the American-backed plan. Even the *New York Times* published an article two weeks before the invasion about how the United States was training an invasion force of Cuban exiles in Guatemala and Florida.

Kennedy made changes that weakened the chances for a successful endeavor. First of all, the landing place was changed from near the city of Trinidad to Bay of Pigs, a swampy area on the southern coast, decreasing the chance of the landing force making a swift advance. Secondly, President Kennedy suspended the second air strike. Without air support, those fifteen hundred exiles from Brigade 2506 were doomed, and they never expected this to happen. They were taken prisoner and were held for over a year while Kennedy negotiated their release.

Youngsters who were in the forced military service were all sent to fight them. Among them were my cousins Chito and Tatoño. We were all afraid for their lives! People who were considered enemies of the revolution—those who could become future leaders of the invasion and the families who were marked as undesirable to the revolution—were picked up by soldiers in trucks and taken to the baseball stadium with their families. Fidel Castro said that if the invasion succeeded, they were all going to face the consequences. He also threatened to leave Cuba on fire if the invasion succeeded, saying they were going to find only ashes. Fidel kept shouting on TV that they were never, ever going to take the island away, telling the people what he was going to do. We were all scared of what was going to happen.

Trucks went through the streets, picking up the undesirable people. When they stopped in front of our house, we could see through our windows. We watched as the soldiers put our elderly neighbors, a retired lawyer and his wife—they lived across the street and were Alina's grandparents—in the truck. One of the soldiers asked the other, who happened to be someone we knew, "And the Barnets?" He replied, "I believe they were already picked up." That was our friend Sandalio, who saved us from having to go through that horrible situation at the stadium. Sandalio's mother and sister were in the process of leaving the country too. His sister was even sent to the same forced labor camp I was sent to in 1968.

Some of our friends who were at the stadium for more than a week told us later on that there were not enough bathrooms for the thousands of people there. They had to defecate and urinate in front of others. Her family made a curtain with their bodies so others would not be able to see them. The smell was unimaginable. They slept on the ground, and children slept on their parents' laps. They were hungry, dirty, and scared, not knowing what was happening on the outside but dreaming that freedom was coming. We were very lucky we were not taken there and didn't have to go through all of that pain and desperation those parents, children, and grandparents went through. They did not even want to talk about their experiences, because they were very painful. Unfortunately, the thought of freedom was gone! The Brigade 2506 had been defeated.

In August of 1961, the country currency was changed, and all personal bank accounts were seized by the government. Out money was worthless, our savings gone! We were allowed to take out only two hundred pesos, which still had some value in some places. My father went to the bank and took out two hundred pesos. I remember how frustrated and distressed he was. People were waiting in line to get their assigned amount out and were upset about their loss. I would have been devastated.

We were young and were not aware of what was coming. We knew our parents were very distressed, and the atmosphere at home was tense. I began to associate with a group of friends that was trying to liberate the country. We were assigned to stick pictures of fish, which was a symbol of the Catholic faith, on people's doors. I went around doing this with friends, but others were involved in other, more dangerous things. I was also selling coupons for the anti-revolutionary cause, trying to raise funds to buy arms. We wanted to bring this government down!

One day, I was carefully passing counterrevolutionary pamphlets to friends at the Ten Cent Store when, all of a sudden, I saw a pair of boots. Someone wearing an olive-green uniform was in front of me. It was someone who used to be my friend but had become part of the system. He grabbed my hands and told me to go home, saying to forget about what I was doing; otherwise, he had to take me to jail. Thank God he did not take me to jail, but from then on,

I was more careful about what I was doing and who I was friends with. I am thankful for those who, even after they joined the government, still showed kindness and care to their friends. Maybe they were sorry they had joined the revolution but could not walk away. Only the Lord knows.

Our home was half a block behind the ten cents store. We lived right in the center of downtown in the city of Matanzas. We could walk to the stores, the park, school, and church. When I got home, I was very nervous, and my mother noticed that something was wrong with me. I told her what happened at the store, and she asked me about where I was hiding those papers. I took my mother into her bedroom, and in the corner I removed a floor tile and showed her where I was keeping those pamphlets. She grabbed them and burned them to ashes. She made me promise I was not going to be involved with them anymore. I promised and stayed away from the group.

Two of my friends ended up in jail. José Luis was sentenced to twenty years in jail, but Armando was sentenced for a year then. They were only sixteen! José Luis spent ten years in prison before they let them go free. Years, later, in 1963, Armando was caught again, and this time he was sentenced to thirty years of jail. They let him out after fifteen years in prison. Both of them are in the US at this moment.

On September 17, 1961, 130 priests were expelled from Cuba and were sent to Spain. This was another big blow to the Catholic Church! What an awful year this was!! During that same year, all the private hospitals and clinics were expropriated, and thousands of doctors left the country. Medical students had to be sent for training in towns and cities in order to supply the medical attention needed at that time. Polyclinics and health cooperatives were formed. Preparations for the **National Health System** began in

1960. The idea was to nationalize the health care system on the island, following the Marxist system. Che Guevara, who was also a doctor, was in charge of supervising this program and was the one working on making this possible.

In 1986, all of those who were AIDS positive were removed from society and sent to segregated camps, away from their families and the population. I used to see an orthopedic surgeon in Miami. His name was Dr. Patrick Barry, and he used to tell me about his medical missions to Cuba, especially to help those who were suffering from AIDS and were interned in those camps. Since 1994, patients who are HIV positive have been sent for eight weeks to a sanatorium as soon as they are diagnosed. In there, they receive training on safe sex and other topics. When this period is over, they return to their communities and work, but if the government finds out that they are involved in unsafe sex again, they are quarantined permanently. I wonder how many of them are accused of this and put away forever?

In the Cuban health system, everybody has accessibility to healthcare, but the problems are the quality of health care people are receiving and the lack of access to medications. The sanitary conditions of those places, including hospitals and clinics, are horrible. On the other hand, for tourists and the government elite, there are hospitals and clinics with the latest technology, which are kept in great sanitary condition. They have access to all types of medications and exams.

Today, the majority of the hospitals are in pitiful conditions, except those for tourists and the government elite. These hospitals are also lacking doctors' services, as more than twenty thousand Cuban doctors are working on missions abroad. The government is paid a lot of money for each of them by the countries they are assigned to.

The **Doctors Abroad Mission Program** is a business for the Cuban government. The majority of the doctors who are sent on missions overseas receive about $2,000 dollars a month. The Cuban government keeps 90 percent, paying them only 10 percent of the amount received. At the same time, the island is lacking doctors while the government is making money out of the enslaved doctors working in other countries. But the image of this is great for the communist government all over the world. The world thinks that the Cuban government has a great heart and immense kindness!

In 1962, the food rationing began. Everybody had to rely on the supplies booklet the government gave them. The government was in control of the rations each person was allowed to purchase and how frequently they were supposed to purchase them.

What's unbelievable is that this ration booklet still exists today! You have to wait in long lines to purchase the assigned product, and sometimes when it is your turn, they've run out of it. Grocery stores, or "bodegas," were empty. Anyway, you could not purchase what you wanted, just what the government assigned you to buy.

Below is a picture of "bodega" before the revolution. It is from my friend Alex's father's bodega, and he is the boy standing next to him.

During that time, there were a lot of Russians in Cuba, and we saw many of them, especially at our city park. We also saw a lot of Greeks on the ships coming into port. Since elementary school, we had been taking English as a second language. Plus, during some summers, we went to a night school to learn English too, because we were waiting for our visas so we could leave the country through the Peter Pan program, and we wanted to be able to speak English. Anyway, I love languages.

We talked to the Greeks and learned about communism for the first time. They were the ones who told my father that communism was taking over Cuba. Greece had once had this system, so they were familiar with what was happening in Cuba. Like at this moment, we Cubans know the steps that this horrible system follows, and we know the symbols that are used, including the red and black flags, the sickle and hammer, etc.

In July of 1962, Soviet Premier Nikita Khrushchev and Fidel Castro reached an agreement to place Soviet nuclear missiles in Cuba. We were not aware of this. However, a United States U2 spy plane confirmed the presence of the missile sites in October of 1962. President Kennedy established air and sea blockades in response to the **Missile Crisis**. The world was on the brink of nuclear war for two weeks before Khrushchev removed the missiles after negotiations. Following this event, immigration from Cuba was then halted by the Cuban regime. About ten thousand Peter Pan children who were waiting to exit—including Marita, Margarita, and I—could not leave the country, and **The Iron Curtain was put into place**.

Our friends Maria de los Angeles and Raul were taken off the plane when they were leaving that morning. Their families were devastated, especially Raul's, as he was going to be fifteen years old and had to go into the obligatory military service until he was twenty-seven years old. He was never able to leave the country, and we never heard from him again. His father was a retired judge from the Batista government.

What was there to do now? We were stuck in a system we disliked, we could not leave, and we were not even able to go to the store to purchase anything, because everything was rationed! Who was going to tell us then that it was going to take us ten more years until we were able to leave the country? Plus, for three years, Pipo and I had to endure forced labor camps! I always think that things could have been worse than they were, and that always gives me comfort. I always think that there are others who had it worse. We were the lucky ones.

Items like toilet paper, soap, toothpaste, deodorant, shampoo, and conditioner were all rationed! When we ran out of them, we had to learn to survive without them. My mother taught us to use baking soda or milk of magnesium for toothpaste and deodorant, and we flossed our teeth with a small piece of thread. Thank God we had those items then, until we ran out. Then we had to find those items on the black market. We did not want to smell bad!

My mother made shampoo out of clothing detergent that was mixed with water. She boiled it and put some lime juice inside to give it a nice smell. We used lime juice or vinegar mixed with water as hair conditioner. We solved the problem with the toilet paper by using old notebooks and magazines, but we had to scrub them to soften before use. My sisters and our friends made fun of this, saying that even our bottoms were well educated! We really had a problem with the soap, though, and there were many times we could not wash. We just rinsed our dirty clothes or tried to find soap on the black market, but it was costly.

Chapter 17

My sister Margarita and her friend Walkiria were going to be fifteen in June of 1962. They always dreamed of having a big party, but at that time my parents could not really afford it. We were all friends because their father had a construction business with my uncle. They visited Ino's home on weekends to play dominos, which was something we did too. We all got together after dinner and had a nice time with them and our cousins. Sometimes we played games, played music, dance, or simply talked.

Walkiria's father talked to my father and convinced him to have both girls' parties together, sharing the expenses so they could have the party they had both dreamed of. He convinced Pipo to give Margarita her party! This was like Christmas. We practiced dance choreography at my uncle's home's carport while the men played dominoes, and we had fun. It took us months before the party to get the dance ready. What a good time we had! It was like we were having a party every weekend. After the party was over, we missed the practices and the great time we had together with all of our friends.

It was a beautiful sweet fifteen party at Las Cuevas de Bellamar (Bellamar Caves). There were fourteen couples wearing beautiful dresses. Margarita received many bouquets of flowers—some were still available for purchase at a few shops—and we all had a wonderful time.

In the family picture, you can see my sister Margarita with my parents, Grandmother Aurora, and our cousin Mayito, plus the rest of my sisters. We enjoyed many other sweet fifteen parties in those years before things got worse.

In 1963, one of my teachers from the accounting school told me that there was a bookkeeper job at the policlinic's accounting office, so I went for an interview. I did not mention anything about our parents securing us visas to leave the country through the Peter Pan Program, nor did I mention anything related to leaving since the iron curtain was in place. I got the job and began working.

I was in charge of helping in the accounting department. I counted the money to pay the workers. These payments were made in cash weekly. I was also in charge of the medical inventory control. We had a room full of the needed supplies for the doctors, nurses, and laboratory and X-ray departments. I made the inventory and sent orders to the government's main supply department to get what was needed. I was also in charge of the statistics, which were all done by hand.

Through my hands, all of the death certificates passed. I noticed many of them saying "death by blood hemorrhage" (muerte por derramamiento de sangre). I began asking and found out that all of these young people were killed by the firing squad. It broke my heart every time I saw the death certificates of all of those young people.

Picture of my first job. With my co-workers Marta, Delia, and Daniel. I was just a young teenager.

Later on, in 1964, I was transferred to the main polyclinic, and there I was also in charge of the petty cash and other bookkeeping jobs, and someone else was in charge of the inventory control. The office manager was someone very involved with the government. He always came to work wearing the olive-green uniform and carrying a gun. This man and I had keys to the petty cash. One day, he knew I was having an audit from the main office accountant department to revise the books. The day before, I made sure the petty cash was in order, balanced with all of the receipts.

The inspector came early in the morning, and the first thing he did was check the petty cash. He knew my family too and knew what kind of people we were. As soon as he finished checking the petty cash, he looked at me and told me I was missing ten pesos from the cash. I told him that it was impossible, as I had made sure everything was in order the day before I left. He asked me if someone else had the key to the petty cash. I told him that the manager did. He told me then that the manager had framed me and to go home at lunchtime and bring back ten pesos to put in the box. He told me not to mention anything to him. I did what he told me to do, and he marked that everything was fine. What an experience that was! I could have ended up in jail for being a thief!

As youngsters, even though the situation was getting worse and many of our friends had already left the country, we enjoyed going to the beach, having musical gatherings at our homes, playing piano, and singing. We always tried to forget the circumstances by laughing, dancing, and just living in the moment. It was then when we learned that some of our friends were government spies. It was a very disenchanting situation not to be able to trust those coming into our home. Under those circumstances, we still continued acting like nothing was happening. We were just careful of who we were going out with and meeting. We had lost our trust.

We still continued going to sweet fifteen parties. One of them was for my cousin Maria Elena, and we had the dance practices over in my uncle Ino and aunt Ina's large carport again. It was a lot of fun with all of us teenagers when we got together to practice for the party.

The picture below is from Cousin Maria Elena's party, which was a beautiful one in our eyes.

Chapter 18

The year 1965 came, and things were getting more tense with those called "gusanos," like "dirt bags" or "scum bags." We were marked because we went to church, dressed nicely, had good manners, and did not wear their olive-green uniforms or accept the communist ideology. This brings to my mind the day we went to the theater Teatro Sauto to see an opera. This time, we sat in the balcony because the mother of a friend of ours was given tickets by someone who was a big shot in the communist government. We were happily enjoying the balcony, watching the opera, but during the intermission, the lights came on, and when some people saw us sitting in there, they began yelling at us, "Gusanos, get out!" We got scared and left right away. At that point, we realized how much hate existed against people like us. It was a dangerous situation. They saw us as enemies of the revolution!

At the beginning of that year, I met Emilio, who was working as a chemical engineer at the Cubanitro nitrogen/sulfur plant. Emilio was from Oriente and had begun working there after graduating from a university in the USA. He was very well mannered and good-looking. He was my first boyfriend. Our relationship did not work. Honestly, I did not like the way he kissed me. I was left with saliva all over my face. What a first kiss!

Then, that same year, 1965, the **Military Units to Assist Production** (UMAP) camps were created. These camps were in the province of Camaguey and were formed for all of those who applied for passports, political dissidents, religious people, gays, and others who were unwanted by the Revolution. The camps' main task was to change these people's mentalities. They were forced to do hard labor, and there was physical and emotional abuse from the soldiers. About thirty-five thousand Cubans were in those camps, which were surrounded by electric fences. Our church priest was sent there, along with many others we knew. These camps were closed in 1968 and were substituted with other camps all over the island. In the new camps, women and men who presented applications asking permission to leave the country were forced to work under the same circumstances. I will talk more about them later on.

In July of 1965, my sister Marita married Rolando, whose grandfather was an American. After the church wedding, my parents had a small family gathering at the house. By then, things were difficult to find, and to be able to have a party, you needed to buy whatever you 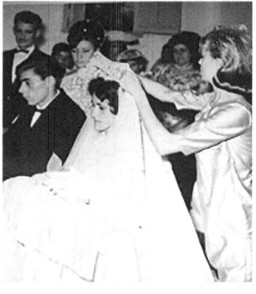 could on the black market, which was costly. My father did that and gave my sister and Rolando a nice reception. They just celebrated their fifty-fifth wedding anniversary!

This is a picture from their wedding. Margarita and I are putting the "mantilla" (Spanish veil) on them. You can see our father on the far left.

It was a sad and happy moment at that time, as our family had been trying to leave communist Cuba for several years, and my parents were afraid that Marita and her husband were not going to be able to leave with our family. Thank God that in 1971, my sister and her four-year-old daughter, Maria Elena, were able to leave with us. She claimed her husband, and he was allowed to join them in a few months. One of the happiest moments!

This was also the year of the **Camarioca Exodus**, and September 25, 1965, was the day that Fidel Castro announced that anyone who had relatives in the United States and wanted to leave the island could do so. Their relatives had to send a claim for their exit and come to pick them up at Camarioca Bay, north of the city of Matanzas. Boys and men of military age (fourteen to twenty-seven) were not permitted to leave. Two hundred thousand people received permission to leave at this time. Immediately, my parents contacted some friends in the United States who had the same last name as my mother, as we did not have any close family member there as of yet. Later on, our neighbors, the Gonzalez family, claimed us as relatives. Because of their actions, we were able to leave about six years later during the Freedom Flights. We are grateful to them for life!

So, I knew it was going to take a while for us to be able to leave the country. I was desperate! I got together with some friends, having had the idea of getting into one of the boats that came to pick up some of their relatives. One of them, José Luis, whose wife was already in the United States, was determined to leave. My friends and I took a bus from Matanzas to Camarioca. While there, the plan was for José Luis to try to get into one of the boats first, and if he made it successfully on the boat, then we would follow him. We were watching him from the bridge, and he was going to signal to us whether it was okay for us to go down to the marina or if we needed to leave immediately. We saw him getting into the boat; he was carrying a lady's suitcase. The government TV camera was there filming this historical event. All of a sudden, we saw the soldiers taking him away, and he signaled for us to leave. We took off from the bridge immediately and went to the bus stop to wait for the next one and go back home.

We were all very nervous and anxious thinking about what was going to happen to him. The next day, we saw on the TV news the moment when he was getting on the boat carrying the old lady's suitcase. We also heard from his mother what had happened to him. He was taken to jail, beaten, taken home, and told him to be ready to leave the country the next morning. They had to let him go because he was filmed leaving on the boat, and he was beaten because he made them look bad for doing so. He made it to the US and was reunited with his wife. In the end, he was the lucky one. All of us were very happy that he achieved his dream of reuniting with his wife, but we were also sad we could not leave. We were lucky we were not caught and put in jail for what we were trying to do.

The boat lift ended prematurely because of threatening weather. Only five thousand of the estimated two hundred thousand immigrants had arrived in Florida. As the boat lift grew more dangerous, negotiations to end it and to establish a safer and more orderly passage intensified.

On November 6, 1965, the United States and Cuba signed a "Memorandum of Understanding," which stated that Cuba would permit immigration and the United States would accept immigrants, with relatives of those already living in the United States given first priority during processing and movement.

The United States further agreed to provide air transportation to Miami for three to four thousand Cuban immigrants per month. The United States established the **Freedom Flights** in 1965. Those are the flights we were able to leave on in 1971. Those flights continued until 1973.

Here is my family in 1965, before Marita's wedding.

We went to the Ministry of Interior on several occasions to check on our status and to find out when were we going to be able to leave. One day, I went with my sister Margarita and saw an officer name Rene. I asked him when he thought we were going to be able to leave. At that point, he stood up. He was very upset and began shouting, "It is going to take you ten years because I just put your file at the bottom of the pile! Leave me alone!" And he was almost right, as it took us five more years to leave the country. Marita, Margarita, and I were supposed to leave in 1961 with the Peter Pan Program, but we could not. Margarita was able to leave via Mexico in 1968, and the rest of the family left in 1971. It was ten years later before Marita and I could leave.

On the way out, I saw my friend Marianela, who had just had breast cancer surgery, coming out of there too, crying. She was a young girl, twenty years old or younger. She was an opera singer who had studied with us at the commerce school at night. I asked her what happened, and she told me that she was begging them to let her go to seek treatment in the USA, as she had been told by the doctors in Cuba that they could not do anything else for her, and she knew there were other treatments abroad. Her family had already presented the necessary documentation for her to leave the country. Unfortunately, the government did not allow her to leave. Months later, I heard she lost her life to cancer.

Chapter
19

In 1966, things were worsening! Harassment, intimidation, and surveillance. That was how it was under the communist regime and its supporters. This made life intolerable and terrifying. People suffered and perished under these communists' laws! Parents were turned over to the government by their children, family, and friends just for expressing disagreement with the system. If you wanted to listen to a radio station from another country, you had to play the radio very low because you did not want to be turned in to the government by your neighbor. My father had a nice radio with low frequency, and we were able to listen to La Voz de Las Americas station (The Voice of the Americas). They were able to update us on what was going on in other countries, especially the United States. That station still exists today, bringing the latest news to Cuba and other nations.

During that time, you were also not allowed to have a TV antenna to watch other channels from other countries, and still today you are not allowed to watch anything but the available communist channels. Actually, when I watch a movie from Hitler's era, it always brings me back to the experiences we endured in Cuba.

All of the freedoms were taken away!
We surely learned to appreciate democracy!

In Cuba, you were allowed to purchase only one pair of shoes a year, if they were available, so by then my shoes had holes in their soles. During the rainy season, I remember my feet getting dirty. My feet would be soaking wet from the water and mud that got into the shoes. It was embarrassing and uncomfortable to be walking with wet shoes and dirty feet when you went somewhere. Also, people had pest problems at home because they could not treat their houses with pesticide. It was not available! We had a rodent and roach problem at home. Roaches would fly in through the tall doors and the windows without screens. We were dealing with having them in our wardrobes and dressers. And mice also got in and ruined our clothes and other things.

One day, I met this guy and began dating him. He was tall and good-looking, and he always had a friendly smile. He told me that he lived in a city about forty-five minutes to an hour away. He told me he was divorced from someone we knew, and of course, we knew they had gotten divorced. He had a car and would come to visit me several times a week. Even though he wore the olive-green uniform, he told my family he was not happy with the government and said that he was trying to find a way to leave the country. My brother-in-law Rolando was planning the trip with him. Rolando had not presented the necessary documentation to the government yet and had not been part of our family nucleus when we applied to leave Cuba. We thought it was going to be difficult for him to leave, so he thought the only solution was to leave illegally. He wanted to live with his wife and daughter in the United States forever!

During that time, you could purchase only one pair of panties a year. My panties had holes in them thanks to the roaches. One Saturday, we went out dancing with my sisters and my mom, and while I was dancing the twist, my rag, which was made out of a sheet my mom cut up so it could be washed and used every month, came out through the hole and fell on the ground. What an embarrassing moment! My boyfriend saw it and kicked it while dancing, and it ended up by a table. People there were wondering what it was. Immediately, I went to our table, sat down, and told my mother I wanted to leave. She was surprised since we had just arrived there.

I would not give her the reason, and we all left. At home, I told her what had happened, and she could not believe we had left the dance. She said that by leaving, people were going to know that it was ours. I told her that I felt too embarrassed to stay there, especially since my boyfriend had seen it when it fell to the ground. I needed to go home and get away from there.

I began noticing that my boyfriend was telling me some lies and that something was wrong with his attitude. A neighbor's boyfriend told me that he knew him and that he was married, and he gave me his address. I knew where he was born; therefore, I sent a letter to the government and asked for his birth certificate. When I received it, it said that he had been married, had divorced, and then he had gotten married again. My sister Marita gave me the idea to take a bus and go to where he was living to see if it was true that he was married. We did that, and when we got there and looked inside the front window of his home, there was a crib in the living room. He was married and expecting a child! When I confronted him with his birth certificate and told him what I knew about him, he blew up! He could not believe I was able to discover the truth. He thought that my neighbor, a retired lawyer, was the one who gave me the idea. I simply told him the truth, that it was my own idea and that I was intelligent enough to know what to do, which was the truth.

At that moment, he told me that he was on a government mission at our home, trying to find out what my family and our friends were doing. He was a spy! He told me that he had one more month to finish his mission there and that if I broke up with him or said something to my parents, he was going to hurt my family and closest relatives who were staying behind in Cuba. It was a very difficult month for me, knowing I had the enemy coming to our home yet being unable to say anything to anyone! Finally, when it was time for him to go, he confessed to me that he was very attracted to me. He said he was sorry but that he had to do his job. What a release it was that he was out of my life forever!

A few months later, I heard he was in prison. What people did not know was that it was his next mission to be among the political prisoners, some of whom we knew, to get information from them. And of course, he let them know that he was my boyfriend and was a friend of my family so he could gain their confidence. One evening when I was standing on our balcony, I saw someone who looked like him standing on the corner. When he saw that I saw him, he hid so I would not see him. Apparently, he was still keeping an eye on us.

This is what has been happening in Cuba all along. People watching people, reporting to the government about any suspicious actions. You could not even trust family members who thought differently from you. The pressure of this situation was unbearable for many, to the point that people started jumping in rafts and boats, or even getting into shark-infested waters, to run away from the Marxist tyranny.

Recently, I heard from a friend who left Cuba to live in Miami, and he said that many of our so-called "friends" were actually government infiltrators watching our movements and what we were saying, relaying information to the authorities that might be detrimental to our well-being. These friends were spying on us everywhere we went. They were trying to detect different ideologies among the youngsters. They were not G2 agents, but they were receiving favors from the government for their work.

He also told me that many of those who had infiltrated our group are actually enjoying their lives here in the USA now. Little

114

did we know that our innocent gatherings at the Liberty Park, parties, the beach, and school became opportunities for them to spy on us. I was also told that they were the cause of me being sent to forced labor camps. And I wonder, are they still spying for the Cuban government in the United States of America? Or do they have it so good here now that they are acclimated to the American ways?

During those years, I was crocheting pantyhose and socks, and Julita was knitting baby socks, caps, and coats, among other things. A mother of a friend of my sisters, whose husband was an officer in the government, ordered socks for her family. I notified her that her order was ready. She invited me to come over and took me into her bedroom. There, she had a statue of the Charity Virgin, and a candle was lit. She was a believer even  though her husband was a "communist." She overpaid me, and I told her that it was too much. Her answer was that she knew we were in need at that moment. Unfortunately, months later, she, her husband, and their mentally challenged daughter died in a car accident while coming back from seeing their son, who was away from home at a camp.

Life was getting so bad that many people were compelled to take the perilous risk of leaving in a raft, venturing alone or with their families or others. We never heard from some of them again. Did they survive? Were they able to get to land, or did they perish in those shark-infested waters? Another thing that was happening was that the only way to bring food to the table was by purchasing it on the black market, which could lead to jail time if you were discovered. Many were willing to risk their freedom to feed their families. Sadly, still today, the government punishes you with jail time for doing this.

My father was not allowed to work anymore after he presented the solicitation to leave the country. We only had a jar of water and some brown sugar in the refrigerator. If we got an orange, my mom made a desert with the orange peel. My niece, who was a toddler then, was crying for milk, and my sister did not have any to give her. The family the government had moved into the downstairs floor of our house kept hearing my niece crying for milk. Even though they were revolutionaries, they had good hearts. They had children there too, and they needed milk for them. One of them told my sister Marita to go with her to a farm, which was where they were getting the milk for their children. Marita finally was able to go with her and buy milk from a farmer. Was this considered a black-market purchase? They continued going to the farm every week to get the needed milk. They were not going to let their children go hungry!

During times like this, our neighbors Chelita and Garcia, the veterinarian, were like angels to us. We will not forget the veterinarian coming to our house on several evenings to bring my father a chicken. He knew that we were hungry and that Pipo did not have the money to purchase our meat quota. The government had put Garcia in charge of the meat market. Chelita sometimes asked my mother to send one of my younger sisters over for dinner. We never forgot their kindness.

116

Chapter 20

After my father presented documentation to leave the country, this made matters worse. Since he could not work any longer, he could not even purchase the quota assigned by the government. We learned the meaning of "being hungry." I remember that in our home's refrigerator, we only had a jar of water mixed with brown sugar to keep us going. I also remember that my mom's aunt Clara came over after walking miles to bring us something to eat once in a while. She was an angel too.

One day in 1966, a soldier came to our house to take an inventory of all of the furniture and electric appliances we had in the house. He informed my father that all of the furniture had to be there, that all of the electrical appliances had to be in working condition, and that his car had to be running when the time to leave the country came. We could not believe this was for real! All of our belongings, including our car, were for the government to keep. They were not ours any longer. We could not give anything to any of our family members who were not able to leave, and if things were broken, we would not be able to leave the country. Unbelievable!!

Even though the situation was getting worse, we still enjoyed going out with our friends. We did our own hair, and since we did not have a blow dryer, we rolled our hair up and waited for it to dry before styling it. We loved to listen to American music, and we were always listening to Paul Anka records, and the Beattles. Later on, the government would not allow people to even listen to English radio stations or play American music. It was the anti-American attitude.

Russians were in control now, and that was the language allowed. You were not supposed to speak in English among friends. Russian was even taught in schools as a second language. If you spoke to the tourists who were coming to the island in another language, you knew that the government was watching you and listening to what you were saying. I was able to communicate in three languages by then and loved having the opportunity to use them, but it became scary and dangerous, and we did not want to do anything to prevent our departure from the country.

While all of this was happening, a friend told me that he was leaving the country and asked me if I wanted to leave with the group. I began planning my trip, but my mother noticed that I was tense and anxious. She confronted me and asked me to tell her what was happening. I told her of our plans to leave in September. She begged me not to do it, asking me to wait for permission to leave legally. I was scared too, so I listened to her and declined the invitation. I told my friends of my decision, and they were very disappointed.

One of them, Edmundo, had suffered years in prison, and his and his family's situation was getting worse every day. They were already marked as counterrevolutionaries. They built a raft in secrecy. My mother was right; it was a very dangerous trip. Their boat began sinking because of the water that had been getting in it. They were forty-five miles away from Key West when they were luckily picked up by a Norwegian ship; otherwise, their homemade raft would have sunk the next day, and they were surrounded by

118

sharks! The ship took them to Norkfolk, and later on they were able to go to Miami, where their relatives lived.

This is the newspaper report of their odyssey.

Rescued in Shark-Infested Waters

6 Cubans Escaped From Castro, But Not Trouble

By CLIFFORD HUBBARD
Virginian-Pilot Staff Writer

NORFOLK—Six young Cubans, grinning after escaping Castro and the sea, came ashore Thursday from the Norwegian collier Breim at the coal piers at Lamberts Point.

They had escaped from Cuba Sunday night and were rescued early Tuesday by the Breim as their homemade raft was sinking under them in shark-infested waters.

The six, admitted to this country as refugees by the Immigration and Naturalization Service, are:

Gonzalo Alfredo Hernandez, 34, a welder.

His brother, Secundio G. Hernandez, 23, a mechanic.

Edmundo Suarez, 31, a draftsman.

His brother, Juan Manuel Suarez, 22, mechanic.

Pablo Camilla Falcon, 27, student.

Angel Lopatgui Castellanos, 23, government clerk.

Edmundo Suarez was the only one in the group who spoke English, and in Capt. Olav Enger's cabin on the Breim he recounted their story.

He was imprisoned three years because, he said, "I was accused of working against the government." He was released two years ago.

"For a year I have been planning this," he said.

Gradually the group, carefully feeling each other out, got together. Six months ago they started building their raft.

The elder Hernandez, a welder, put his trade to good use. They built the raft of steel.

Hernandez, with the help of the others, made two steel pontoons. Then they built a platform on the pontoons. The job took approximately six months of secret night and weekend work.

"I cannot tell you where it was built," said Edmundo Suarez. "There are others."

They placed two outboard motors on the stern. "In very bad condition, both," said Edmundo.

Last Sunday night from a spot apparently near Matanzas, the

(See 6 Escape, Page 6)

Edmundo Suarez (third from left) and Capt. Enger pose happily with the five other refugees.

In August of 1967, my sister Margarita and I received visas to leave the country via Mexico. My sister Margarita and her boyfriend had been dating for several years. He was able to leave Cuba through Mexico, and in order for him to help get us out, he married my sister, got the necessary paperwork, and claimed her as his wife and me as his sister. Aunt Marta, who was already in the United States, was going to pay for our airfare. During the bus trip to Havana to get the visas, Margarita and I were very anxious and happy, dreaming about finally being able to get out of that hell together and go to Mexico, then the USA, and we were hoping to get the rest of the family out later on. We were so hopeful and glad we were going into the unknown together and that we would be able to help those left behind.

When we got to the embassy of Mexico in Havana, the gentleman who took care of us denied my visa. He said that he was not my blood brother but my brother-in-law; therefore, he could not claim me. We were devastated. Margarita did not want to leave Cuba alone. She wanted me to be with her; she did not want to face the uncertainty of traveling to Mexico alone. On the way back home, we were silent, wanting to cry but holding in our tears.

When we came home and informed our parents of what happened, we all cried. We had to convince her to go, reassuring her that she was our way out of there. She unhappily agreed and was able to leave in April of 1968, though she was worried about what was going to happen to us. Aunt Marta paid for the place where she was staying, which was a place that belonged to a Cuban lady. It was a large house, and the lady rented its rooms to Cuban refugees.

It was there where my cousin Mayito stayed when he left alone. Aunt Marta and Mamama stayed there when they left through Mexico. While Margarita was living in that house, her "husband" decided to divorce her because he wanted to begin his new life in the United States alone. Their marriage was never consummated. Two years later, she was able to leave Mexico, and she went to Worcester, Massachusetts, where my grandmother Aurora, Aunt Marta, and her son Mayito were already living.

In 1967, the Marxist government implemented programs at the secondary and pre-university levels. They were called the **Brigades of Working Students,** and for students attending the university, they were called the **Brigades of Social Work**. These students had to live in remote, rural areas for one month at the beginning of this program, but later on, the length of their stay was changed to forty-five days away from their families, doing agricultural work on state farms and in cooperatives. Parents had to gather food to take to their children when they visited them on Sundays, which was difficult for them to do due to the rationing, gasoline shortage, and transportation. If a student did not go to work in the fields, he or she was not allowed to continue studying anymore; this happened to my sister Margarita. And the Marxist government tells you that education is free!

After many years of these programs, in 2011, the government realized that this system did not work, as none of the students knew how to do this type of work. Instead of helping, this was hurting the country's agricultural production. It was also becoming too costly for the government to send all of those students to those farms, especially when the food shortage and transportation had been becoming critical on the island. It was becoming very difficult to provide these students food; plus, they had the expense of housing all of them. They were causing more damage to the government than good; therefore, this program was ended.

This was my last picture before I was sent away to the forced labor camps.

Chapter 21

It was January 1, 1968. The dreaded long speech of the communist dictator Fidel Castro was getting ready to begin. The Committees of Defense of the Revolution had their speakers ready on all of the blocks, waiting to force the people to listen to him even though we hated it. Usually, his speeches lasted for hours, and that loud noise was like a sermon with no end.

Then, on January 13, there was another speech at the Closing Cultural Congress in Havana. During his discourse this time, Fidel mentioned us: the undesirables, the counterrevolutionaries, the ones who wanted to find freedom in other lands, the "gusanos" (earth worms). Fidel said, among other things, that those who wanted to leave the Revolution could not do it so easily. They would have to pay with their sweat to get out of the country. They would have to work in the fields and farms to pay the Revolution for their exit from the country. We were astonished! What was going to happen to us? What was his plan? Who was he going to send to these forced labor camps? That was the talk among those who were waiting to exit the country. The only thing left was to wait and see what happened.

In February of the same year, we met a guy from Czechoslovakia who was working as a chemical engineer at the Cubanitro plant in our city. He was happy because he had heard that the people in Prague rose up, trying to get rid of the rigid communism there. He was going back to Prague and was thrilled with the news. Here is Karel with Margarita, our dear friend Lourdes Mayra, Mirtica, and me.

Unfortunately, President Dubcek's efforts to establish a more humanistic communism that would be celebrated across the country, called **Prague Spring**, was brief. On August 20, 1968, the Soviet Union invaded Czechoslovakia. This uprising was finished, and the communists continued dominating the country. We were wondering what happened to Karel under these circumstances. We never heard from him again.

Rumors also said that people who disagreed with the government were being sent to forced labor camps. It had already happened in Cuba in 1964 with the UMAP (**Military Units to Aid Production**) forced camps for the undesirables. They had been taken at gunpoint to unknown places, where they were forced to sign a document declaring themselves scum of the society, and later they were taken to different concentration camps in the province of Camaguey._

People from all religious denominations were sent to the UMAP camps too. You were marked as undesirable just for practicing any religion! A friend of mine was sent to this camp because he was a Jehovah Witness and was considered dangerous to the new system. He was forced to march for hours, day and night, with a rifle attached to his body since he refused to hold it, and there were other atrocities they were forced to do.

The nuns had already been exiled to different countries, and the priests were sent to this camp. Our priest at the cathedral then, Fr. Jaime Ortega, was sent there too. He eventually became Archbishop of Cuba later on in life, holding that position until his death last year. Several priests came from Spain and were assigned to the churches the priests had been sent away from. In a communist system, you can be persecuted for believing in God, and Cuba was declared an atheist country. We continued our involvement at church, though; we sang in the choir and kept our religious life the same. They could not take God away from us, nor could they take our beliefs or our faith.

The Marxist doctrine that Fidel Castro was imposing on the island brought programs to the school level too, as I mentioned before. The mandatory **Brigades of Working Students,** which began in 1967, were in full action. Kids as young as twelve years old were forced to go to rural areas, away from their families, to do agricultural work during the months of February, March, and April. At this time, Julita and Mirtica had to go in order for them to continue their education and finally graduate.

They were placed in barracks, one for the boys and another one for the girls. At that young age, being away from their parents, kids got involved in sex. Some were raped, and many accidents occurred. Since the media was completely controlled by the government, none of these events were ever reported by them! Also, remember that abortions were available even without the consent of their parents. Along with that, since these youngsters did not have experience doing agricultural work, they caused damage while doing their farm work. In 2011, this program was finally abolished.

While in there, Julita and Mirtica stuck to their group, and a friend brought some holy hosts from church. They took communion on Sundays, hiding in the bathroom so they were not seen by the guards. Away from their families, those students had to attend workshops organized by the people in charge of the brigades, and

124

they were indoctrinated into Marxism. They were told that they were doing that for the good of the Revolution.

Castro's worldwide political propaganda said that schools were free, but children and adults receiving an education had to pay their way through school by working in the fields. The only positive thing about this program was that at least these children were able to have meals. Many could not have meals at home because of the food rationing imposed by the government. They endured farm work during all of their high school years. Those attending college had to do the same thing through different brigades; otherwise, they could not graduate.

Meanwhile, back at home, we had been waiting for the dreadful day when we would be sent to these forced labor camps, but we thought it would only be my father. In June, we received two letters from the government, one written to my father and another one to me. It was very upsetting when we found out that I also had to go to one of these camps.

We had to be ready to leave for the camps on June 20, 1968. They told us to bring only working clothes, that they were giving us the working boots. The letter informed us that we had to be at the Plaza de la Vigia by 9:00 a.m. It did not state where they were taking us, but it said that if we were not there, we had to face the consequences of our actions, as not being there meant that we did not wish to leave the country any longer.

My mom—who was taking care of my two smaller sisters, Mirtica and Julita—and my oldest sister Marita—who was already married to Rolando and had a baby named Maria Elena—were not sent to the camps. Rolando was not sent because he did not have any documentation to leave the country that he could present to them, and he was still working. Margarita was lucky that she had previously left for Mexico; otherwise, she would have had to endure those hard labor camps too.

They asked us to pack working clothes. I did not have any working clothes! My father gave me two of his long-sleeved shirts, and I also had two pairs of socks, a kerchief, and a pair of old jeans. A neighbor gave me a hat, and I used an old backpack for everything else, like my toothbrush, my comb, a rubber band to hold my hair up, and some baking soda to clean my teeth and use as deodorant, because I could not leave my family without toothpaste and soap, which were things that were already rationed. Mima was going to see if she could exchange something for soap and toothpaste for the next time we came home. They gave me a pair of boots, which I had to return when I left the country.

Chapter

22

When we got to the Plaza de la Vigia, where Sauto Theater is, there were about ten buses waiting for us, and there were about five hundred people or more waiting to get on them. We were separated. My father went with the men, and I was sent with the women. There were women of all ages, and I found many of my friends there too. My mother and sisters were devastated, especially my mom. She was upset when she saw us leaving, not knowing where they were taking us, what was going to happen to us, or when we were coming back. We loaded the buses, and I could see family members crying. I could see the desperate look on my family's faces when the buses were leaving. My mom was waving, but I could see the anguish in her face. The men were taken to a farm in Camaguey, many hours away from where we lived.

After our buses departed and we spent several hours riding, the women were taken to Cejas 2, a farm in the middle of nowhere. It was in the city of Pedro Betancourt, not too far from the town called Navajas, which was in the province of Matanzas. I was familiar with that town because my grandfather's brother Enrique Barnet was the chief of the train station in the town of Navajas for many years, which was not too far from where we were taken. Uncle Enrique was already dead, though. When we were younger, we used to go with my aunts Irma and Mirta to visit their uncle, aunt, and cousins there, and we always had a nice time.

When we arrived at this huge farm, the buses crossed through a very high chain-link fence, and we were brought to a group of barracks where armed soldiers were waiting for us. There were about three hundred women of all ages at that time, but later it grew to five hundred women when the rest of the women arrived from all over Matanzas. We were instructed on what to do and what not to do, and we were given a number, though I no longer remember mine. We were assigned to different barracks according to the number they gave us when we got out of the bus. My barrack was made of wood walls, and there was a palm fronds roof. There were open windows that had loose burlap bags covering them, so all kinds of flying insects and animals got in. The doors were guarded by soldiers of both sexes. There were lines of bunk beds, and burlap bags were used as mattresses. Thank God I brought a blanket and my pillow. My sisters had told me that I was going to need them. But I didn't have a mosquito net, and I really needed one there. I was especially afraid of the scorpions because I had been bitten by one as a child.

I was assigned to a unit where I did not know anybody. I don't even remember the name of the lady who was staying in the upper bed. She was not very friendly. It was better if you had a friend with you so you could share the anguish of being away from your family, your home, and your life. Even though I am a very friendly person, these women were so involved with their own pain that they did not open up to others. I guess they were afraid since they did not know anyone, and under that regime, we could not trust anybody, as a spy could be among us, reporting our conversations. Besides, there was not a lot of time, as we had to work and work, and at the end of the day we were so exhausted that we did not feel like talking to anybody. We just wanted to go to bed!

We were all quiet, wondering what was coming next, already missing our families and homes. Some of the young ones were crying, and I felt like crying too, but because I was so upset, I couldn't. I was very angry and felt so impotent. Finally, I fell asleep.

I was angry about the injustice that was being committed by the government. They were forcing us to be there, away from our families! There was no reason for the government to force us into those labor camps! I was angry because I couldn't run away or scream at those soldiers to let them know the pain they were causing all of us. I was very angry with that repugnant communist government, and what made it worse was that I could not express my feelings. We had to accept the reality and survive, dreaming of being free one day.

After we brought all of our belongings in, guards whistled for us to form lines in front of the barracks for a roll call. We were called by our assigned numbers. Then we were taken to the dining area, a building with no walls that next to the kitchen. It had tables and benches with enough room for all of us. Some of the older women were assigned to work in the kitchen and the dining room, and the rest of us were assigned to work in the fields.

We were served a miserable dinner of pea soup with weevils inside, which we put aside while eating, and after that we were taken to another open barrack with an old television set, where we could see only the government channel. At least we had something to entertain us at night. At 10:00, we were sent to bed, and all of the lights were turned off. Then people started crying.

The bathroom was a horrible experience! Before going to bed the first night, I needed to go to the restroom. Well, there were latrines where we had to squat over a hole in the ground. There were no walls, so everybody could see what we were doing. There were no lights at night, and besides that, we needed to bring our own toilet paper, which was something that was already on the rationing list. The sinks to wash our hands at were in a different place, and we also had to bring our own soap, deodorant, and toothpaste, which were very difficult to find on the black market.

There were several of those latrines for our use, and we had to wait in line most of the time.

The next day, after a day of hard work, all of us wanted to take a shower. I waited my turn, and when I went in, I saw that there were open showers with no curtains, so everybody could see me naked! I have never, ever taken a shower surrounded by naked women. We all got together and made the decision to take some old sheets and divide the showers so at least we could have more privacy. By

the end of the week, the bathroom's floor was full of filthy water that went up to the ankles, and we had to walk through it to use the latrines or to take a shower. It was stinky and disgusting!

Every day, we had to wear the same sweaty, smelly clothes since we needed to save our soap and water. I used to hang mine on the side of my bunk bed to dry the sweat, and the lady sleeping in the upper bunk used the other side to dry her clothes. The worst times were when we were menstruating. We had to bring our own sanitary pads because they did not provide us with any. We were on our own during that time, and we had to solve our problems the best way we could.

At home, we were six women with no pads. We could not find them anywhere because the government was not providing them anymore. My mother solved this problem by taking an old bedsheet, cutting it into pieces, and dividing it among all of us. Each of us had our own set that we had to wash and reuse. I brought a set to the camp for when this time came. When it did, I could not wash them and ended up throwing them away. What was I going to do when I needed them again? My mother decided to exchange some items for pads so I could bring those pads with me to the camp, and at home I used some of my sisters' and boiled them.

I never had a doubt that all of this sacrifice and misfortune was in the name of the freedom we were dreaming about every day! By the way, Marita and my mother did a great job potty training Maria Elena, so we were able to use her cloth diapers as rags, which were more absorbent. Each of us got a set that we kept in our personal nightstand drawer. They were much better than the bedsheet rags we were using. Since the soap supply was short, sometimes we could not even wash them, so we had to rinse them and boil them, and that did not work sometimes. Yuck!

Around 5:00 a.m., we were whistled and told to leave the barracks and to stand in line to go to the dining room for breakfast. We only had ten minutes to drink the dirty water they gave us for breakfast! We were given a little bit of coffee. It was made out of chickpeas that were roasted in a pan to give some color to the water, and there was a little bit of milk inside. That was all! Then some of us proceeded to the wagons, which were being pulled by oxen to take us to the fields. Others were taken by trucks. It depended on where you were working that day. We started working at 6:00 a.m. and continued until dark.

Summers in Cuba were hot! The sun got very strong, and the heat was so intense, making it unbearable to work in those fields. We were divided into brigades and were assigned to different working areas and different working tasks. One day, mine was to cut malanga strings that we had to put into a sack. Malanga is a type of root vegetable grown in the Caribbean. The part of the plant that is eaten is the tuber, similar to a potato. They told us that the strings had to have a specific length, and we had to have one hundred of them in the sack, no more and no less; otherwise, they would punish us by making us work longer hours in the field. That happened to my group when one of the communist leaders named Manuel counted them at the end of the day, and we had to stay until we had one hundred in each sack (some sacks had eighty or a little less than a hundred). You can lose count easily!

When lunchtime came, we were again given a pitiful meal of yellow grits with weevils (gorgojos) inside. We were so hungry that we just pushed them to the side of our plates and kept eating. After that, we had to go back to the fields to continue the same task. If we were working in a field that was far from the camp, they brought the lunch to us, and we just ate with our dirty hands. If we needed to go to the restroom, there were none. We just went into the woods to do whatever we needed to do. To clean or dry ourselves, we

used leaves and tried to clean our hands with them too. At least they were providing warm drinking water, though many times there was dirt at the bottom of the large canteen. We used the same cup! Nobody was worried about catching any sickness!

I remember when I was in another camp and we were picking guavas around Camarioca River. We were able to drink its cooling water. We got the water when it passed over a rock, so we did not get the tadpoles. The water was fresh and cleaner than what they were offering us in that dirty container. When you are hungry and thirsty, you do what you need to do to remedy the feeling. We were also able to wash our hands and faces during lunchtime. They brought us a can with whatever they made in the camp, usually chickpeas or beans and a piece of bread. At least we were able to rest for a short while. When they were not looking, we ate some guavas to kill the hunger. I lost so much weight that I went down to ninety pounds!

Thank God someone had a camera, and we were able to take these pictures as a testimony of what happened there. Who was going to tell me that I was going to be working on the land that belonged to my ancestors? They had been able to sell the forty hectares before Castro got there. Anyway, the government confiscated all of that beautiful land.

Almost a month later, we were informed that we were going to be allowed to go home on Saturdays every two weeks so we could do laundry, and we were to be picked up on Mondays. In my case, I got picked up next to the park. It seemed that they could not provide the water for all of us to keep our clothes and ourselves clean. Maybe we were too smelly! We had been wearing those sweaty, filthy clothes for too long!

That Saturday, when they let us go, we had to find our own transportation back home. This camp was about two hours from where the majority of those women lived! We all ran to the road to find a good soul to give us a ride home. My home was more than two hours away from there. The majority of the rides we got were from truckers. Sometimes we just sat in the open truck bed, without railings, hoping the driver did not make any sharp turns. We were dropped off somewhere in the city of Matanzas, and we had to walk home. Sometimes it was a longer walk than other times, but we were happy to at least be able to be at home for the weekend.

When I got home, my mom was so surprised and happy I was there. We embraced and cried. She didn't know what to do or say! We just embraced. I asked about my father, and she told me she hadn't heard from him, either, but the rumor was that they were fine. The men were not allowed to leave camp like we were. My mother could not believe how thin I was! She made me a good dinner with whatever she had in the house. I rested for a while. My bed felt so good that I just wanted to stay there, talking to my sisters, telling them how things were.

Later on, we went over to my aunt's house to see if we could exchange some things that we had for the extra things she had. She was able to exchange some sugar for a tube of toothpaste that I took with me to the camp. From there, we also went to Ino and Ina's house, thinking that maybe I could get something to take back with me, but they didn't have anything. On Sunday, we went to church, and all of my friends were glad to see me. I also went to the park, a place where the youth met on weekends. Some of my friends did not want to even speak to me. Since I was already marked by the government as undesirable, they were afraid of being marked too.

On Monday, at 4:00 a.m., we had to meet by the park to be picked up and taken back to the camp. As soon as we got there, we were taken to the fields to work from 6:00 a.m. until dark. After dinner, I would go to the barrack where the TV was, and since I had brought my crochet needle and thread this time, I continued making net pantyhose and socks until I was sent to bed. That was the way I was helping my mother with the house expenses. She was able to buy the government-assigned quota of groceries. This kept my mind occupied too.

134

After being there for almost six months, I began having uncontrollable diarrhea and could not eat anything. My weight went down to eighty-five pounds. I was sent home sick. They did not want the others to contract whatever I had. Again, I had to find my way back home. The next day, my mother took me to the polyclinic, and the doctor informed me that I was having some kind of stomach virus and gave me permission to stay home for a week. He also told me that I had a bad throat infection and that I needed to have my tonsils removed. My thyroid problem was getting worse without medication, and all of this was causing me to have depression too. But I felt like I was in heaven with my mom's attention, resting, sleeping in my bed, and recuperating. Only the Lord knows how much I missed home! The week went fast, and I had to go back to those enslaving labor camps.

Again, we were taken to the fields early in the morning. Later in the afternoon, it seemed it was going to rain. This time, we were cleaning the field with machetes and cutting weeds. It began thundering, and we were all worried about lightning since we were using machetes. The rain began to pour down, and we were told to stay put in the field and to continue working. The guards were inside the cab or under the bed of the truck, protecting themselves from the storm. The soil got wet, and our boots began collecting soil in their soles. It became very hard to walk. Soldiers were laughing and making fun of us, watching all of us get soaking wet. We were very scared that we were going to be struck by lightning! It didn't matter to them! We were their slaves, and they had control over us.

Finally, we were called back to the truck and were taken back to the camp. The feeling of impotence was overwhelming. The rage of seeing them laughing at us made my hands into fists. What could we do about this? If we wanted to be able to leave this communist dictatorship, we had to do what they told us to do or stay in Cuba forever! The next day, our clothes were still humid, but we did not have any other choice but to wear them again.

I heard that a year later, when I was not there anymore, women went on strike due to all of the abuse they were going through. The chief of the Interior Ministry came to talk to them and agreed to make some changes, but if they wanted to leave the country, they had to continue working in the fields. Those women went back to work, and those soldiers became somehow more humanistic, but some abuse still continued.

After six months away in a camp in Camaguey, many hours from Matanzas, my father was allowed to come home to see a doctor. He had tendonitis that was caused by cutting sugar cane, and he needed hand surgery, followed by therapy. He was not able to work for another four months, but he was sent back again, this time to a camp in the province of Matanzas, just a few less hours away. He was able to come home once a month on the weekends to do his laundry.

My father was very skinny, sunburned, and depressed, and it was pitiful to see him like that. My poor mother had to deal with all of our problems, but she was lucky to have our brother-in-law Rolando living with us. He was the only one working at that time, but he had to support his wife and daughter. It was not an easy situation. My mother was able to sell some of our personal things that were not in the government inventory so she could buy the food quota at the "bodega."

One day, one of our friends came over and offered to help us sell perfume on the black market so we could make some extra money and support the family. At first, my mother said no, that she was not going to risk going to jail and losing her freedom. We convinced her to let us try with our girlfriends who we knew were in the process of leaving the country someday too. She also approached members of our family to see if they were able to purchase some. She got the perfumes, and we began doing that.

Of course, we smelled very nice, and one day when we were passing by the house of Caridad, the president of the Committee of Defense of the Revolution, she stopped us and asked us why we were smelling so nice. Aunt Marta had sent us an Avon perfume sample that Mima had cut into smaller pieces and put them into smaller bottles that we had, adding alcohol to extract the smell of the perfume. When Caridad wanted to know where we got the perfume from, we were already prepared. We knew that this was going to happen. We took her to our home and showed her what my mother had done with the Avon sample, and we offered her one bottle. Of course, she took it, and that problem was resolved, thank God.

Chapter 23

Every day was the same at Cejas 2 Camp, until one special, horrible day. We were coming back to the camp, and I was with about other nine women in this wagon. When we got to the camp, one of the girls jumped off of the wagon and unfortunately fell on top of one of the posts of the picket fence. She was impaled by the sharp fence post, which penetrated the inside part of her thigh. The bleeding was tremendous, and she had to be rushed into one of the trucks and taken to the hospital for care. We never heard about her again, and I did not even know her name. It was a very tragic moment that I have never forgotten. We were all crying and were traumatized from seeing this unfortunate accident happen. That night, I could hear some of the ladies softly crying, and others were talking about what had happened. I just stayed still, thinking about that moment, wanting to cry aloud, but I just stayed still, looking at the bottom of the cot above me.

The next morning, we had to be ready for the morning roll call in front of the huge barracks, and then we had to run and get some coffee made of fried peas, then go to the wagons. I continued getting sick at the camp, and one weekend when we were sent home, I was so sick that I could not report to camp on Monday morning. Instead, I went to the doctor again. He said that I needed to have my depression treated. On the same block where I lived, across the street, was Dr. Ariel, the director of the psychiatric hospital. My neighbor spoke to him and asked him if he could see me. I went with my mother to see him at his hospital office, and he prescribed a bunch of medications and gave me a health certificate recommending for me to stay home until I got better.

Dr. Ariel was also giving lessons at the local university. He needed someone to help him prepare his lessons, and since I already had my teaching degree, he asked me if I could help him with them. He was not paying me, but I did it anyway. One of the neighbors had a key to his apartment, and he told me to ask her to open it for me while he was working at the hospital so I could go in there and get the books I had to read in order to prepare his next day's lesson plan.

One day when I was returning the books, he was there, and he told me that I looked tense and nervous. He pointed to the sofa and told me to sit down. I sat down, and he began massaging my shoulders, and then he told me to lie down on my stomach. He began to massage my back. All of a sudden, he began touching me in an inappropriate way, and I did not like that. I tried to get away but could not. I felt penetration, followed by a tremendous pain. I screamed, but he continued and continued even though I was begging him to stop. He was about six and a half feet tall and was heavy. I could not get him off! When it was all over, he just simply told me, "At least I respected your virginity!"

I felt humiliated, dirty, and guilty for being so naive and believing he was helping me as a doctor. That doctor's health certificate helped me to stay away from the labor camp for a while, but it caused me too much suffering and pain! It took me twenty-five years to be able to speak about this horrible incident. After all of this happened, I began having uncontrollable migraines, especially on weekends, when I could rest from the labor camps. I threw up constantly, could not be around light, and had to stay in bed until it was over. I think they were caused by tension and nerves.

Meanwhile, Dr. Ariel had a huge problem at the hospital. He allowed his mental patients to use machetes to cut cane, and some of them began threatening others. Another one ended up on top of a tall palm tree, and it was very difficult for the nurses to get him down. Finally, all of the patients were controlled. He was dismissed from his position and sent back to Havana, where he was from.

A few months later, his mother came to pick up his things from the apartment. She came over to our home and told my mother that Dr. Ariel had suffered a massive heart attack and died. He was in his forties, and she was devastated that he had passed away so suddenly. In a way, I felt sorry for his mother and young son. For him, I felt he received a punishment for what he had done to me, and who knows how many more young women he was treating this way.

I went to see another psychiatrist at the polyclinic, and he could not believe that I was given all of those medications. Dr. Ariel had kept me drugged! This new doctor had to get me off of those drugs little by little to detoxify me. The new doctor's report to the government said that I could return to the fields, but I had to be sent to a mobile unit so I could go to sleep at home.

Even though I was happy that I was able to go home from camp every day, at the same time, I was saddened by the attitude people I knew had toward me. Many of my "friends" began giving me the cold shoulder, ignoring me, and staying away from me. It was hurtful in a way, but what helped me was keeping my thoughts on the upcoming future. The idea of freedom was stronger and kept me going. We also were very active at church and were part of the Cathedral Catholic Church Choir.

Before I was sent back to camp, I had a friend who expressed his love for me. He was called Pepito "Khrushchev" because his father was a very well-known communist. Pepito followed in his father's steps and was also a communist. He was a very good-looking young man, was well mannered, and was the only child in his family. He was also a poet and told me that he wrote many of his poems about me. He used to come to the park, sit with me, and read his poems. I knew I could not fall in love with him. I knew that if I did, I would not be able to achieve my freedom and would have to stay in Cuba forever. Besides that, I was not going to deny the existence of God!

One day in 1969, I was coming back from the fields. The truck always left us by the library, which was located at one of the corners of the central park, a few blocks from my house. I used to walk across the park and take the sidewalk by the Ayuntamiento, the beautiful government building, and walk two blocks to my house. I began walking on the sidewalk, and suddenly I saw Pepito coming toward me. He stopped me and began talking to me, and I told him that my friendship was going to hurt his image with the Revolution. He told me that he was very involved with the Revolution, that nobody from the government could hurt him because he was a communist by conviction, and that those were his beliefs before Castro's Revolution. He began by saying that I looked beautiful, even with my dirty clothes. He also told me that he needed to speak to me that night after dinner. He was going to come to the door of my house. I told him it was okay and that I was going to wait for him.

After I took a shower and dined, Pepito came to my house's door. He did not want to come upstairs, but he invited me to go to the park. We walked to the park and sat on a bench. He grabbed my hand and told me about his desire to marry me, saying how much in love he was. I thanked him for his feelings and gave him some examples of what could happen if we got married. The first thing I said was that I was a Catholic and that he was a communist. I was going to continue being a Catholic, and after having children, I wanted my children to be baptized, to go to church, to believe in God, and to practice the religion. I knew that was against his principles and beliefs; therefore, we could not get married. He knew then that he was not going to be able to change my beliefs and that I was not going to be able to change his. He realized that our love was not possible even though we liked each other. We were compatible in many ways, but not in our beliefs and principles. He took me back home and kissed me on the cheek.

Years later, when I was married and pregnant with my first child in the USA, I was watching TV, and suddenly a channel from Cuba showed up. It was a program where Pepito was describing and presenting a film that was going to be shown. I could not believe my eyes! I told my husband, Bob, about him and how in love he was with me. Years passed, and then I heard on the Spanish TV station about an Italian airplane falling down in Italy; all of the passengers had died. Pepito was a famous TV personality in Cuba then, which was why his death was announced on the news. I was sorry for his passing. He was a good man despite his principles and beliefs.

When I was transferred to another unit, we had to be at the park at 5:00 a.m. to be able to get on the truck that was taking us to the camp. The first mobile unit was to a coffee plantation in the hills of La Cumbre, on a farm called La Conchita, a place not too far from home. There were men and women working together, but at least the food was a little bit better. At this farm, men dug holes with a pick through the furrows in the hills of this mountain, and women put the coffee grain in the holes. I believe this was in 1969.

I remember seeing these men digging into the hard terrain, and all of a sudden we heard screams coming from the side of the hill. A man was on the ground. It was our city doctor, Dr. Arnold, and he had had a heart attack. By the time they got him down the side of this mountain to the camp, he was dead. He left behind a wife and five children. They were all friends of ours. My sisters and some of his daughters were going to school together. He wanted freedom for his family! Unfortunately, his older son reached the military age of fifteen years old. Their mother decided that the entire family would stay in Cuba instead. One of his daughters, Tania, came to the United States with her family. The rest of her family joined them between fifteen to twenty years later. Sadly, Tania died from leukemia last year. Her younger brother decided to stay behind in Cuba.

Later on, I was transferred to another unit at a farm in Guanabana. It was called Corral Nuevo. There, I had to clean the weeds from pots, making sure I did not remove the real plants. I met nice friends there, including Magda and Aixa. Magda's boyfriend, Fito, was already in the United States. She counted the days until she could see him again. We were told that if we removed the plant, we would be accused of sabotage and would be sent to jail for conspiring against the communist revolution. You needed to know exactly how the plant looked so you did not confuse it with the weeds, and you also needed to clean the plastic bag where the plants were. We did this while sitting on a very low bench that my father made, as these black plastic bags were on the ground.

We spent hours sitting there under the sun, finding baby rats, snakes, and other creatures when we moved the bags. It was scary at times because we did not know what we were going to find. I developed callouses on the bottom of my cheeks from sitting for so many hours and doing that labor on the hard bench! The dirt was so embedded under my nails and cuticles that even when

I had a manicure done, I could not get the dirt out. My face was sun burned, and my hair was dry.

One day, at the end of a hard workday, we were informed that because the truck that was supposed to take us back had broken down, we needed to find our own way back home. At this camp, one of my neighbors, Jazmin, was also working with me. At the main road, we had to ask for a ride. Suddenly, someone stopped to pick us up. He left us at the entrance of a military base on the highway. We needed to cross the highway so we could find another vehicle to take us home. When we all began crossing, a military jeep came out of the military base so fast that it hit Jazmin, and she went flying in the air, landing on her side. We all screamed and ran to see if she was okay, and she was in a lot of pain. She had a big cut in her right arm, and we could even see the bone.

The ambulance came and took her to the hospital. We were all shaking and had to continue looking for a ride home. We finally found someone to leave us at the park near my house. Later on, I found out that Jazmin was released from the hospital, and she only broke her arm and got stitches, thank God. She could not work; therefore, she was relieved from her duties, and a few months later she left the country. It was definitely a very scary episode.

One day, the camp's officer came and told the group of women that they needed volunteers to be moved to another mobile unit, which meant we would have to go to different places to work. There were about twenty of us, fifteen men and five women. My friend Aixa encouraged me to join her, Julia Luisa, Nancy, and others and leave this unit. I was so sick and tired of spending the entire day sitting on the small bench that I decided to accept.

144

We were sent to Punta Hicacos, north of Varadero Beach. We had to plant pine trees in front of the beach, making a wind barrier. Beside that barrier was the saline plant. Where we took the trees from was an area full of mosquitos. They could bite you through your shirt! The first day was unbelievable, as we had not brought any protection.

The second day, we cut a piece from one of our mosquito nets at home, and I was able to wear it under my hat, covering my face, neck, and shoulders. But still, those suckers were getting our blood! In that area, we were able to see the beautiful tiki homes the government was building for tourism. They were very rustic and had access to the beach. I guess they had to do something about the mosquitos, because they were fierce. We planted all of the wind barriers in Punta Hicacos.

Another time, I was sent for a week to fertilize pineapples in a camp away from home. Only six women were assigned to go there, and we stayed at this camp for a while. This happened a week after I had my tonsillectomy done. The person in charge did not care about the letter my doctor had given me to present to them. I just had to go or lose my right to leave the country.

My friends Aixa and Julia Luisa were also sent there with me. We had to fertilize a field of pineapples, and those needles at the end of the leaves pinched us constantly. They did not give us any type of protection, but we used our head kerchiefs to cover our mouths. We really were glad when this assignment was over.

Below are some pictures of this mobile brigade. In one of them, I am fixing Aixa's hair. The only advantage was that we did not need to be sitting down under the sun for so many hours. I was so glad I accepted the new task and joined them!

It was the best choice I made. This brigade had a less stressful work environment. Even though we were always under the surveillance of the government people, we still laughed and did the best we could to make the hours go fast. Aixa, Julia Luisa, and I sang trying to entertain the group, and this singing in open fields caused me to develop callouses on my vocal cords. I had to have a special treatment so I wouldn't lose my voice.

Aixa and I have kept our friendship all of these years and are still in touch with each other. I have seen Julia Luisa at some parties of the Matancero Ausente (Absent People from Matanzas), but I never heard from Nancy or any of the other guys again. I still remember all of the hard work we shared and all of the support we received from those men. We even got support from the government ladies and guys who were watching us, making sure we were doing our job, of course.

They even let us take these pictures, and some posed with us. They were farmers from the area, and I guess they did not have any other choice but to join the system. Remember, all of these farms were confiscated, so all of those farmers were displaced and had to work wherever they could. I am also sure that there were others who would do anything possible to hurt you in the name of the Revolution. We were their enemy!

In October of 1969, the **"Ten Million Sugar Harvest"** began. Workers and students had to "volunteer" during their free time to cut or plant sugar cane. At that time, religion and religious celebrations were abolished because they were considered counterrevolutionary actions. Christmas celebrations were banned from 1969 to 1998, and this period was called **"The Silent Christmases." December 25 became a regular working day.**

Cubans were not allowed to put up a Christmas tree or anything allegoric to this celebration. Parents were only permitted to purchase one basic toy (up to ten pesos) and two additional, cheap ones at the beginning of January. In Cuba, children received their toys on January 6 in celebration of the Three Kings Day, when they brought toys to baby Jesus. A year later, the date was changed to July 26 in celebration of the Revolution.

In 1992, religion restrictions were loosened, and Catholics and other religious groups were even permitted to go to church and join the Communist Party of Cuba at the same time. Castro began describing Cuba as a secular country instead of an atheist one. Finally, in 1998, after Pope John Paul II visited Cuba, Cubans were allowed to celebrate Christmas as a holiday again. Almost thirty years later!!

Chapter 24

In 1970, Margarita called us from Worcester to tell us that she had a boyfriend named Frank, who was from Las Villas, and she had met him over at my aunt Marta's house. He was one of our cousin Mayito's friends. It seemed that she fell in love with his beautiful blue eyes. She told us that they were planning to get married pretty soon. Margarita began working at the same factory where he was working.

In June of the same year, they were married. My mom cried from both happiness and sadness. My parents and all of us were happy but sorry that we could not be there during that important

moment of her life. After the church wedding, the reception took place at my grandmother's house.

We prayed for this marriage to be a good one and wished her all the happiness in the world. We were happy they were in love. She called us after the wedding, and we spoke to them and wished them all the happiness. After fifty years of marriage and three children, they are still happily married.

We continued our lives in Cuba, Pipo and I going to work in the fields. My mother was taking care of my two younger sisters, who were attending their last years of high school, and Marita busy with her toddler, Maria Elenita. We were wondering when we were going to be able to leave that hellhole! On weekends, we always tried to plan some fun to forget about all of the trouble. We went with friends to house parties and to the beach, or we just played the piano or cards, trying to entertain ourselves and not to think about the reality of our situation.

On June 21, 1971, when I was coming back home from the camp in the truck, I noticed that the truck did not go on the same route it usually went on; instead, it was going toward where I lived, and it stopped right in front of my house. To my surprise, everyone in my family was outside the house, and some neighbors were surrounding them. I noticed a government seal on the front door; it said we could not go into the house anymore. My mother began yelling, "We are leaving! We are leaving!" I took off my hat, my head kerchief, and my mochila and gave them to the women in the truck. Everybody cheered! I got out of the truck and was embraced by my mother and sisters. We cried from happiness. I asked her, "What am I going to wear?" She told me that she had made sure I had at least two changes of clothing.

Then we had to wait for my father to come home from the camp he was assigned at. I could not enter my house anymore! It was a homeless feeling. There was uncertainty and emptiness, but at the same time, we were happy that our dream of leaving that dictatorship was going to happen. We went to our granduncle Secundino's house, which was at the corner of ours, and it was there where I took a shower and got rid of the dirty, filthy clothes I had been wearing in the fields. Our cousins from the neighborhood of Nara-

149

njal came to say goodbye, and other neighbors did, as well. We could not sleep that night!

The next morning, I had to go back to the camp where I was stationed to return the boots the government had given me. There was Chief Raimundo, the one who would come up next to me on his horse when I was working in the middle of the fields and yell, "That's the way I want to see you, bitch, (perra), full of dirt!" As I was leaving his office, I said to him, "You are going to continue eating dirt while I am going to be free and will eat well!" He yelled back, "That can cost you your exit out of the country!" I continued walking toward the car and left without looking back at that hellhole.

That afternoon, my father, my mother, my sisters, Maria Elena, and I left for the airport. It was a very emotional moment because our brother-in-law Rolando was staying behind, and we did not know when he was going to be able to leave and see us again. Mima, Pipo, Marita, Rolando, and Maria Elena rode in my uncle's car, a 1958 Chevrolet, and Julita, Mirtica, and I went in a friend of mine's car, which was a 1959 Cadillac that had a long tail. We called those cars "cola de pato" (duck's tail). Our cousin Tatoño rode with us too.

We spent that night at the airport and had some ham sandwiches for dinner. The next morning, when we were ready to leave, the soldiers took our passports after stamping them with the word null (nulo) and kept them. The only identification we had were our birth certificates and baptism documents. My father had them in an envelope, ready for our exit of the country. All of that money that we spent in those passports was wasted. Here is my passport picture.

150

We left on the Freedom Flights organized by the US government, after the Camarioca Exodus from 1965 till 1973, and as soon as the plane took off, the pilot said, "Welcome to the USA!" We could see the island in the distance, and everybody began singing the Cuban National Anthem. We were going to be free at last! The stewardess came by and asked us what we wanted to drink. We all asked for a coffee, and she asked, "With cream?" Thinking it was going to be a café con leche, I said yes, but the rest said no, thinking it was an expresso coffee. When we got our coffee and tried it, we all looked at each other, realizing that it was not the coffee we were expecting. We could not drink it! Today, I prefer an American coffee with cream and sugar over an expresso.

In the blink of an eye, we were in Miami. It was a beautiful view from the air. We were very surprised to see so many boats and white houses. When we went through immigration, we showed them our birth certificates and told them what had happened with our passports. It took us hours at customs, and in the end we each were given a green card. From there, we proceeded to the buses that were waiting for us inside the airport, as we did not have any close relatives in Miami to pick us up.

These buses took us to a place where all of the Cuban refugees were taken. It was the Freedom Tower. In there, they took us to a bedroom that had three bunk beds. Maria Elena slept with her mother. We all shared the bathroom. The next day after breakfast, we were told to go to the basement. There, they had tons of used, donated clothes. They gave each of us a coat, a pair of boots, and other winter clothes, as we were going up north. All of this was possible thanks to the donations of the Catholic Relief Program.

I asked someone who was near the phones for a dime to make a phone call, and he gave me two. We called our family in Worcester to let them know we were flying to the Boston airport on June 24.

Then we called the other phone number we had, which was Margarita's ex-husband's family. We told them that we were in Miami, and his brother came over later on that evening and took us to a shopping center. We could not believe what we were seeing. So many beautiful stores full of nice things available for purchase, but of course, we did not have a cent!

He bought my younger sisters a pair of shoes each and let other friends from church who were living in Miami know that we were in Miami. Other friends came to see us the night before we left for Boston. They brought us some gifts, which we really appreciated. Some of them had come to the USA just a few years before us, so they were still adjusting to the exile life and were working very hard to have enough to support their families. We were very glad they came to see us there.

Several years later, we found out from my mother's uncle Secundino, who lived two doors from us, that after we left in 1971, the police came looking for Julita to take her to jail. If this would have happened while we were there, that would have been a devastation for the entire family. Thank God we were able to leave when we did. Our enemies' plan did not work, and they were too late. The Lord was with us!!

Chapter 25

T he next day, we took the plane to Boston, Massachusetts. We knew not to order coffee, so we got sodas this time. My family  drove a few hours to meet us at the airport. When we were able to reunite with them, we were so happy to be all together again, and to our surprise, Margarita was pregnant with her first child. We were all thrilled. I could not stop smiling from happiness. My brother-in-law Frank's family came to meet us too, along with Mamama, Aunt Marta, Mayito, and some of their friends.

Pictured above are Rolando, Marita and Maria Elena, Mima, Pipo, Mamama, Mirtica, Margarita, Frank, Marta, and Nery. Julita is not in the picture because she took the picture.

Six months later, after our arrival, Marita's husband, Rolando, joined us. He was claimed by Marita. Thank God he was able to come and reunite with her and his daughter sooner than we expected. He was very lucky. He left behind his mother, father, and the rest of his family, but his older brother was already in the United States.

At the airport, we said goodbye to Aunt Irma and her family, as they were living in Union City in New Jersey. We promised we were going to visit them as soon as we were established. We rode in two cars, one driven by Frank and another one driven by Mayito. Chito drove my aunt Irma and her family back to New Jersey. He was living in Newark, not too far from Union City. Chito's wife, Magaly, and his children were still in Spain.

When we arrived in Worcester, my mother, father, Marita, and Maria Elenita stayed with my grandmother and Aunt Marta. Julita, Mirtica, and I stayed over at Margarita and Frank's home. Even though my grandmother and aunt were happy to have all of us finally free, they were also saddened because the day after our arrival, our cousin Mayito left after being drafted into the Army. Marita and her family found an apartment in the same building where our sister Margarita was living. We found one in the building next door, and our grandmother was living in the building on the corner across the street. We were all living together on the same block!

As soon as we arrived in Worcester, a social worker sent us to an office to pick up a box of groceries, and they gave my father a check to assist him in finding a place to live. As political refugees, we had a different consideration, and the Catholic Bureau was also guiding and helping us. My father told the social worker that what we were needing right away were jobs. He did not want any handouts! He began working in a local factory, and my mother worked in another one. Marita was taking care of her daughter, and my younger sisters were attending high school. I began working with Aunt Marta at Adam Street Bilingual School as a teacher's assistant. Marta was a Spanish teacher there. I also began going to a satellite school of Amherst University. We were all also taking English as a second language classes.

When we moved to Miami, I began working as assistant to the comptroller at Maru Distributing Company. At the same time, I went to college at night and received my bachelor's degree in education in 1974. I left that company in 1975 and began teaching at South Dade Skills Center. Later in life, after being married for about five years, I went back to school at night to study for another degree, and I received my master's degree in diagnostic teaching in 1981. Then Bob went back to school too and received his master's degree in vocational education. I thought about becoming a school administrator; therefore, I went back to school and received the specialist degree in school administration and supervision in 1989. However, I decided to stay in the classroom until I retired in the year 2000. Anyway, Bob and I worked together at the same school and lived only ten minutes from work.

Our son Bobby visited Cuba in 2018, and this is what he wrote about what he experienced:

"I've been swimming in feelings since I returned from Cuba. (And I'm listening to Gloria Estefan as I type this!) It's a country that simultaneously felt familiar and foreign to me. I also feel more connected to my family's experience of leaving their home and all of their possessions behind to go to a new country that was unfamiliar to them. My Cuban family came here with nothing but the clothes on their backs, barely speaking the language. This photograph was taken shortly after my mother arrived in the USA forty-seven years ago. In the photo are my grandparents, my great grandmother, my aunts, and my uncles. She said they were wearing hand-me-downs. But you can still see the light in my mother's face. As is the Cuban way, you figure it out. You do what you have to do to survive. If it weren't for their experience, sacrifice, and determination, I wouldn't be here. I'm so grateful to my mom, my family, and my roots.

And I'm proud to be an American."

In the above picture, whoever took it missed Marita carrying Maria Elenita, who was sleeping, as well as Julio, my aunt Irma's husband. They came with their two children, Julio Antonio and Zoila, who was the same age as Maria Elenita. Then there is my sister Margarita with her husband, Frank; my mother; my grandmother; Cousin Chito; Pipo; Aunt Marta; Mirtica; and me. Squatting are Julita and our cousin Mayito.

More of what Bobby said:

"During the trip, I met so many wonderful Cubanos who have the drive, ambition, and ingenuity that was instilled in me all my life. They sadly don't have the same opportunities on the island that we have here in the USA. That's what's so great about this country: You can come from a foreign land, as many of our ancestors have, and take advantage of the opportunities that are available here. We have so much to be grateful for."

156

Here are pictures of Bobby standing in front of the door at our house when he visited Matanzas. We lived upstairs and it is awful to see how deteriorated the balcony and doors are now. Also, we never ever hung clothes on the balcony. We had a clothesline in the interior patio. Things have certainly changed for the worst.

Because of those thirteen years that we lived under the communist dictatorship, I learned to mistrust people in Cuba due to all of the circumstances we went through. When Bobby went to Cuba, I was a nervous wreck, thinking that something could happen to him there and that we would be forced to go to Cuba to deal with the situation. Even though our son Marc would like to visit Cuba too, he does not want to upset me by doing so. He knows how scared and worried I was when thinking about what could happen to his brother there. I don't trust that government. You can be accused of whatever and, for no reason, be put in jail.

Chapter
26

Julita got married in February of 1972 in Worcester, Massachusetts, to an Ecuadorian gentleman named Milton. She was only eighteen. They went to live in Miami, and in August of the same year, my mother, Mirtica, and I went to visit them. When my mother was there, she made the decision not to go back to the cold weather, and she asked my father to move to Miami. My father accepted, and I went up north to help him pack our things and sell the furniture we had so we could begin our life in Miami with only $500. Immediately, we looked for jobs, and we all began working within a week. We rented a house, and that is how we really began our lives in the USA.

A year later, in 1973, my two sisters Margarita and Marita moved with their families to Miami too. They rented their houses just a block away from my parents' house. Mirtica and I were single then, living with our parents. Julita was only a few miles away, and her first son, Javier, was born there. Her second son, Milton Jr., was born four years later. Julita and Milton got divorced after fifteen years, and she never got married again.

Some friends from Cuba used to come over on the weekends and visit my parents, especially Juan, who was getting divorced. One day, he confessed to my father that he was in love with my sister Mirtica and wanted to marry her. They were married at a Masonic temple when she was only eighteen years old. They got divorced after thirteen years of marriage. Later on, when her daughter Vivian was almost fifteen and her son Ricky was five  years old, she met an American guy named Jack, who was a young widower, and they got married a year later. They are still married after thirty years.

This is a picture of Mirtica and Jack's beautiful Catholic church wedding.

In 1974, we all purchased our first houses with our first Florida refund income tax checks in Leisure City, a neighborhood north of Homestead, Florida. These houses were surrounded by a nice lawn, and we purchased them one next to the other: my parents' house, then Marita and Rolando's, then Margarita and Frank's, and then Julita and Milton's. Mirtica and Juan's house was one block away, at the end of the street.

Since I was the only one still living with my parents then, I gave them the down payment for our house. In that neighborhood, Marita had a son named Guillermo in 1975. Maria Elena, who was born in Cuba, had already adjusted to school. Margarita had her son, Frankie, and two daughters, Lillian and Liset. Julita had two sons, Javier and Milton. Mirtica had a daughter, Vivian, and a son, Ricardo.

I left my parents' home to get married.

At the gas station where we all purchased our gas, the manager was a young American guy named Robert Kircher. He was very nice to me. One day in 1975, he invited me to go out for a lobster dinner that Saturday, and I accepted the invitation. That Thursday afternoon, I was going to the doctor, and he found out that I had a cyst in my breast that needed to be removed. I had to cancel the lobster dinner with Bob because I had to have an immediate lumpectomy done the next day. Thank God it was normal. I called Bob to tell him how sorry I was that I could not go out with him. He sent me flowers to the hospital and brought me a box of chocolates when he came to visit me at home. From there, he began visiting me every day. We got married in 1976. We purchased a home in a neighborhood called Princeton, where my mother was selling houses, not too far from my family.

While living in that house, we had two sons, Robert Jr. and Marc, and both make us very proud. Thank God we are still married and hopefully will be until death do us part.

When our children were ten and eleven, we bought a five-acre farm in Redland, an agricultural area between Miami and Homestead. We had two dogs and two horses, plus a 6,090-square-feet house that needed constant attention and maintenance. We purchased this house from the US Marshals, which turned out to be a great investment. After Hurricane Andrew in 1992, with the payment we received from the insurance, we hired people to fix all of the damage done by the hurricane. At that point, we realized we were paying too much in taxes. We decided to buy another property. I had always dreamed of having a place right on the beach.

Therefore, in 1994, we decided to buy a condo right on the beach in Marco Island, which is on the southwest coast of Florida and is just an hour-and-a-half drive from Miami. We enjoyed using it, but we rented it during the winter season to snowbirds from the north. We still have it!

This morning, here at my home in the United States of America, I was watching the news about the drought in Africa, and I saw people in line trying to get water. This took me back to Cuba, to Castro's dictatorship. We lived in the upstairs of a hundred-year-old house (no water pump). The city water pressure became so low that the water would not reach the upstairs. We had to go around the neighborhood to beg for drinking water. My father got a big, open tank and placed it on the patio to collect rainwater. We used that water for bathing, flushing toilets, cleaning, laundry, etc.

Now, looking at the problem with immigration, it reminded me of what my sister Margarita experienced when she left Cuba and went to Mexico. She was there for two years while waiting to receive her American residency. Remember, the Mexican consulate denied my visa, so she had to leave alone. While being there, she had to report every week to government officials and sign. She could not work, and if she did, she risked the Mexican government finding out and sending her back to Cuba. Under those circumstances, she had to obey the immigration laws of the country; otherwise, she would have been deported back to Cuba. This happens in all of the countries in the world. She could not risk her freedom! It took us years to legally enter the USA and become political refugees.

We have the same rules here in the United States, but now it seems that some people want to change them. Thanks to our Aunt Marta, who was working very hard in a factory in Massachusetts. She was the one paying for all of Margarita's expenses during that time in Mexico (God bless her). We were in Cuba and did not have the means to help her in Mexico, as all of our assets had been confiscated by the communist Cuban government, and my father and I were suffering and were working in those forced labor camps by then. By the way, Margarita sent me the thread I was needing to make the pantyhose I was selling to support the family.

Now that so many years have passed, I reminiscence about our life in Cuba, the good and the bad moments. We are very proud of what our family has accomplished in this Great Nation that gave us the freedom we were lacking in our own country. We all achieved the American Dream through education, hard work, and taking advantage of the opportunities offered to us. We are proud of all of our children, who also achieved the American Dream in the same way.

Our parents used to dream of one day being able to see Cuba free. Unfortunately, they were not able to fulfill their dream, but it is our dream now too. You can plan ahead all that you want, but life can change your plans and your direction in an instant. Thank God we are a family of faith, and that was the reason we lived through those terrible times. I always say, "Others had it worse!"

My parents had the enjoyment of seeing all of their daughters get married in church like they wanted. They were very proud of all of our accomplishments, our families, and our children. They were able to be with us during all of the celebration parties the sisters had in their homes when our children were growing up. My husband, Bob, always said that we had a birthday party every weekend!

In the first picture are the proud parents and their five daughters in the USA years later.

In the next picture, standing are Anel (Marta's granddaughter); Maria Elena, who came from Cuba; Aunt Marta; Mima; and her grandchildren Frankie, Javier, Guille, Bobby, and Milton. Squatting are my parents' granddaughters Lily and Liset, and Marta's granddaughters Adiris and Amarys are next to Pipo. Then there are grandchildren Ricky, Marc, and Vivian.

My parents were very happy to have a big family.

Thank God for my dear close family: Bob, Bobby and Marc.

We are very thankful that we were able to come to the Land of the Free and give our children the opportunity to be born in the United States of America. Even though we are Cubans, we feel for the country that gave us the freedom we lost in our own.

Special thank you to our parents, who worked very hard in the United States of America to achieve the American Dream. They left us two houses that were completely paid for when they died. It is unbelievable to think that Mima and Pipo accomplished so much in so little time.

It is almost impossible to believe that so many years have passed since 1959, and still today, in 2020, Cuba is ruled by the horrendous communist dictatorship that has ruined the country in all aspects. It has separated families for generations.

People are suffering from hunger, and the country's economy is devastated, while the government elite live the life of the rich, making millions, traveling the world, and purchasing properties in many other countries.

We, the Barnet sisters, still hope that one day we will be able to go back and see again the place where we were born, and we hope to see it free.

We are thankful for all of the kindness from the people we have met. I am especially thankful that I have had the support of my family, especially my sisters (pictured above), while writing this book.

The Lord blessed me with a wonderful husband, and I am thankful for him and our two wonderful American sons.

May the Lord bless you and us all, and may the Lord bless the United States of America.

Acknowledgements

To my husband, Bob, for his suggestions and corrections and for supporting me during the writing of the book.

To my sisters, Marita, Margarita, Julita, and Mirtica, for reviving my memory and allowing me to use their pictures in the book.

To my Aunt Marta, for helping me with the memories of our ancestors and sharing some of the pictures used in the book.

To my son Bobby, for allowing me to use the reflections he wrote about his trip to Cuba in 2018 and for allowing me to use the pictures he took while visiting there.

To my friends Magda Alfonso, Marta de Armas, Aixa Hernández, and Magaly Padrón, who shared their experiences during the time we were together in those forced labor camps.

To my friend Estela Fernandez, for refreshing my memory about the time we shared together in Matanzas while going to school.

To Alex Arguelles, for letting me use the picture of his father's grocery store in Matanzas, Cuba.

To my friend Ana Leon, for giving me a helping hand with my picture.

To HavanaTimes.org/opinion/Cuba, for the students in the field report.

To TheRealCuba.com, for their informational pages.

To Wikipedia, for fact-checking information.

About the Author

N ery was always telling her immediate family about what she went through during those years under the communist dictatorship in Cuba. They wanted her to put it in writing, and it took her years to come up with this book, as the memories were very painful at times.

She was born in Matanzas, Cuba, and came to United States in 1971 on the Freedom Flights, along with her parents, her sisters, and her niece Maria Elena. In 1983, she published a book of poetry called *Algo de mi (Something from me)*, which included poems she had been writing since she was fourteen years old. She is in the process of finishing a short story about the year her father was in and out of hospitals and rehabilitation centers, which led to his death. It will be titled "Diary of a Dying Father."

Nery is also a music composer and has participated in several festivals, including Festival OTI of Miami, where her song was one of the finalists. She also participated in the ACCA (Association of Critics and Commentators of Arts) music competition, where she received second place for one of her songs, placing after her mother, Elena Maria, who got first place.

She has been a dedicated volunteer through the Civitan International Service Organization since 1988. She has formed many Civitan Clubs in Florida and Junior Civitan Clubs at different schools in Miami-Dade and Collier Counties. Internationally, she and her husband formed the Civitan Cancun Club in Mexico and the Mount Everest Civitan Club in Nepal.

Made in the USA
Coppell, TX
02 July 2022

79499234R00096